A Collection of

GHOST
STORIES

THE WORLD'S MOST HAUNTED LOCATIONS
AND PARANORMAL ENCOUNTERS

VOL II

H.J. TIDY

CONTENTS

INTRODUCTION

There is nothing more interesting than a good ghost story. For generations, we have gathered around campfires, huddled at sleepovers, and whispered in cemeteries about the stories we have heard, especially those which have terrified us. So many of us are addicted to the rush of a good horror tale, and we find spooky stories the most fascinating. However, many feel the best tales told are the true ones, and that is what this book is about. Exploring the truth behind famous myths and legends is just as interesting as the fictional —and sometimes even scarier.

It is infinitely more engaging to hear about first-hand accounts of the paranormal, especially when multiple people have experienced the same events. It is also more believable, as the stories become part of supernatural lore and history. By drawing on the facts of the stories, it is easy to discern what is fact and fiction and further explore the world of the supernatural.

The stories in this book will explore distinct narratives, all of which have several eyewitnesses who experienced the same ordeals. While it was often a primary individual who was involved with the sighting, every story has other witnesses to corroborate what the primary individual has experienced.

Some stories are gruesome, while others are psychologically terrifying. One of the most intriguing parts is that they happened to real-life people, some of whom even lived to tell the tale themselves. This book is not here to convince you of the supernatural or even make you believe the stories, but to entertain with the real-life accounts of these people. You may even change your mind about what you believe.

In this book, eight distinct and different accounts of the paranormal will be told, making for some of the spookiest stories in North America. Stories filled with witnesses, and some even with physical evidence; each one engaging in its own way. So please join me as I delve once again into the world of haunted locations, paranormal experiences, and demonic possessions.

CHAPTER 1
AMERICA'S GREATEST GHOST STORY

S tories of witches, the supernatural, and ghosts have existed for centuries. Even before the advent of written language, people whispered these tales to one another. They traveled far and wide. Interest in the supernatural is among the oldest aspects of human society.

For the greatest ghost story in American history, we need only cast our minds back to the 1800s, where the story of the Bell Witch began. This supernatural occurrence originates in the town of Adams, Tennessee, and is entrenched in Southern mystical history.

Since tales of this apparition began, many have believed in its existence. Countless individuals have come forward with their experiences, and feel they have proof that she exists.

There is a mystery surrounding who the Bell Witch is. There are many theories. However, it is difficult to distinguish fact from fiction. It is particularly tricky as this happened so many years ago, and those who went through these experiences are long gone.

Like with any supernatural story, some are dubious of how legitimate these eyewitness accounts are. Some have attempted to debunk the narrative and prove that it is nothing more than folklore. It is difficult to have the full picture of what is true and what is hearsay. As always, I am not here to convince you of what to believe. I simply want to tell you the story of the Bell Witch.

How much you believe is up to you.

Note: This story briefly mentions sexual assault in the third section. Reader discretion is advised.

THE LEGEND OF THE BELL WITCH

This legend begins with the Bell Family, who moved to Tennessee in 1804. They lived on a farm in Robertson County and experienced many trials and triumphs in their time together. While one of their children died at a young age, the rest flourished, marrying and having children of their own. Zadok Bell became a prominent lawyer and Thomas Gunn, a successful farmer (Tennessee State Library and Archives, n.d.). The women of the family married well, which was very important at the time. Unfortunately, the family also experienced the horrors of being haunted by a vengeful spirit.

The history of the Bell Witch herself began in the family home in 1817. The Bells noticed strange phenomenon around the house and farm, which they could not find the source of. They saw strange animals roaming the area and heard unexplained noises coming from different parts of the house. It soon became apparent to them that a supernatural entity was making itself known.

They eventually made contact with this ghost, who revealed herself to be an evil entity sent to torture the family. Their neighbor, Kate Bates (sometimes referred to as Kate Batts), was the one who purportedly performed some sort of dark magic as retribution for a family feud.

The first historical documentation that references the existence of the Bell Witch comes from the year 1820, in the form of a journal entry. This was written by John R. Bell, a military officer who stopped by the residence one night for dinner. While there, the family told him about what was happening to them. He wrote of the daughter's experience, stating, "A voice accompanies her, which says she should marry a man, a neighbor–thousands of persons have visited her to hear this voice." (Fitzhugh, 2020).

There is even a story of President Andrew Jackson, who allegedly stayed at the property for just one night.

His plan was to remain there longer, but he left after one night from the fear he experienced. He later said, "I vow I would rather fight the entire British Army single-handed than face this witch again." (White, 2004).

Who Was the Bell Witch?

The prevailing theory of the witch's identity supports the Bell family's story that the entity was, in fact, sent by Kate Bates. Some believe this relates to a woman who lived in a nearby town that quarreled with John Bell, the Bell family patriarch, and cursed them with dark magic by summoning a spirit to their house. The dispute was over land, and Kate felt as though John Bell was attempting to cheat her while making a deal. Kate was reportedly often heard saying that she would get even with John, and spoke of this even on her deathbed.

Some also believe John murdered Kate due to the torment she forced his family to endure. Others posit the idea John murdered Kate first, and then she came back to punish the family.

It's difficult to know what is true and what isn't. The records kept in the 1800s are not clear. Some have been lost; others never existed. Perhaps we will never know what really went on between Kate and the Bells, though that might be why the story is so intriguing.

Where is the Bell Witch Now?

Following John Bell's death in 1820, a mere three years after the haunting began, the sightings of the witch became few and far between. In fact, the spirit seemingly disappeared for seven years. The children who remained on the property claim that she came back in 1827, behaving exactly as she had before. She vanished once again and did not reappear until 1935, when the entity returned to haunt descendants of the Bell family (Tennessee State Library and Archives, n.d.).

In the last few decades, people have claimed to have seen the witch at the former Bell home. The sightings are rare. However, those who witness this supernatural being are often terrified for their lives. This is no peaceful spirit; this is something born of dark magic that intends to frighten and harm the living.

Despite the reduced sightings in recent years, the story of the Bell Witch still fascinates people. Movies such as *An American Haunting* and *Bell Witch Haunting* have been made based on the narrative, and people still research the history, hoping to find an answer to what really happened.

While the history of this haunting tale is interesting, the events of the haunting are absolutely shocking.

DISTURBING ENCOUNTERS

Since her first appearance in 1817, the Bell Witch has made herself known to many people. This spirit torments those who encounter her and instills fear into the hearts of all who visit the former Bell family home. Even though some seek her out, they acknowledge that seeing her is a terrifying prospect.

The Bell Family

It only makes sense to tell the story of the Bell family's encounters first. After all, they are the first ones to have ever encountered her and seemingly the reason she was summoned in the first place. And, of course, the entity was named after them.

As mentioned before, the first supernatural sightings on the property involved strange animals roaming the farm. The family first saw something they assumed was a rabbit. However, upon closer inspection, they found something much larger and stranger. They likened it to some sort of hybrid of a rabbit and a large dog (Fitzhugh, 2013).

Strangely enough, it was John Bell's daughter, Betsy, who was the prime target of the haunting. It was Betsy that John R. Bell referenced in his journal entry, and it was her story that garnered the most attention. At the time of the witch's appearance, Betsy was madly in love with her betrothed, a man named was Gardener.

The pair planned to marry as soon as possible, and by all accounts, the family and community were happy with this marriage. There was support for them to be together, and they loved one another very much.

However, this seemed to anger the witch greatly, and she set her sights on ensuring this union did not take place. She began by whispering to Betsy at all hours that she was not to marry Joshua. At first, this was harmless, and she simply ignored it. Then, the spirit became violent. The witch endlessly taunted her and physically abused her. Betsy was battered and bruised from these episodes. Wherever Betsy and Joshua went, the entity followed. It hunted them mercilessly. Eventually, this all became too much for Betsy, and she called the engagement off.

In addition to the mystery of why the witch was so angered by the presence of Joshua Gardener in Betsy's life, there was also another suitor vying for her hand. His name was Professor Richard Powell, who had been Betsy and Joshua's school teacher. He was eleven years older than her and was secretly married to another woman. Some wonder if the witch thought he would be a better match for young Betsy. If this was the case, she got exactly what she wanted. Betsy married Richard and they moved to Mississippi. For Betsy, this was the end of her torment.

The family also experienced the classic signs of a haunting. There were never-ending banging and clunking sounds with no explanation, and beds in the house were pulled apart. Sounds rattled against the windows and walls for hours on end, and the Bells were driven mad by the never-ending ruckus. The entire house shook at times. Some family members, like Betsy, were physically harmed. They would be bitten, pinched, and have their hair pulled. Sometimes, these attacks went on for hours.

Lucy Bell was the only family member who was treated kindly by the witch. The entity would sing to her when she was in the shower and would care for her when she was sick. There seems to be no reason why Betsy endured so much and Lucy was spared, though how could we possibly make sense of a witch's thought process.

It is also speculated the witch was the cause of John's death. He was gradually poisoned, which led to his passing. Many believe that the slow and painful circumstances were the result of dark magic.

William Porter

One of the more famous stories of the witch's interactions with another human is the tale of William Porter. He was a family friend of the Bells who lived only a short distance from their farm. William and the spirit became well acquainted, and he had no reason to fear her. He referred to her by her name, Kate, and he feared no harm from her. The witch, however, eventually struck. One freezing night, Kate asked to lie in William's bed. He heard her say she wanted "to spend the night with him and keep him warm" (Wick, 1987). William told her that if she wanted to sleep in his bed, she needed to behave herself, and Kate agreed to these terms. She did not keep her word.

That night, while William was sleeping, Kate pulled the covers from off him, exposing his body. He awoke to her crawling closer and closer to him. As this was happening, he had an idea. Rather than panicking and forcing her away, William moved to grab the spirit and wrap her in the bedsheets she was on top of. He then ran to throw her into the fire, hoping to burn her. Unfortunately, he was unsuccessful. William claimed that as he approached the fire, the weight of the entity got heavier and heavier, and that a horrible smell came from the bedsheets (Wick, 1987). He had to drop the witch and run for his life into the freezing outdoors. The legend goes that Kate never asked to spend the night with anyone ever again. This story is so well-known that one of the most famous illustrations of the witch is of William Porter attempting to burn her. It was drawn in 1894, many years after the incident, which shows just how important this event was to the lore of the Bell Witch.

Enslaved Persons

The Bell Witch famously had a vendetta against the enslaved persons at the Bell family property and tormented them relentlessly. She would not only taunt them at all times, but would often physically hurt the men and women at the farm. The witch had her sights set specifically on one enslaved person named Dean, who needed to carry protection with him to fight her off. He claimed that the spirit did not come to him in her human form, but rather as an animal. When this happened, she appeared as either a wolf or a dog; sometimes it had two heads, sometimes none at all (Tennessee State Library and Archives, n.d.).

There is no reason why the witch would go after these people. Some have proposed the idea that she was a bigot, though once again, there is no way of knowing.

Robert L. and The Shakers

In 1988, Robert L. and his band, The Shakers, were recording a song about the Bell Witch. It was titled "Living in the Shadow of a Spirit" and was born from Robert's childhood fascination with the legend of the entity. It became a four-song EP, as a single tune could not hold the entire story of this myth.

Robert visited the property many times with many people to gain knowledge about what the location was like. There was a cave nearby where townspeople often spotted the witch, and Robert thought this would be a great place to capture just how the people of the 1800s were feeling during her most active years. One such visit was with his girlfriend on a beautiful day. While in the cave, she turned and asked him if he could hear a noise. It was the sound of a woman singing at the far end of the cave. It was an ethereal sound. After listening to the noise for a while, Robert says the sound began to affect him physically. "It was an eerie sound that made us weak in the knees and it went on for a couple of minutes" (Fitzhugh, 2013). This was the only supernatural experience he had in the cave, but it was enough to spook him.

The Filming of The Bell Witch Haunting

When filming *The Bell Witch Haunting* movie in 2003, the crew of the film had quite a few experiences they recall as being quite strange. Ric White, the director, recounted hearing a strange voice while in the same cave that Robert L. had visited. He was there with a writer for the movie, exploring in silence when they both heard a voice saying, "What are you doing here?" (Fitzhugh, 2013). They looked for the source of the noise but could not find the person who had spoken to them.

After filming and editing the movie, there was another incident. The office where the completed movie was stored spontaneously caught on fire. The origin of the fire was a fax machine that had been in the office the entire time. The team used it often and normally left it on while they weren't there. By all accounts, there was nothing wrong with it. Why it burst into flames was a complete mystery.

Luckily, Ric had a copy of the film at his home and was able to re-edit the footage there. While working, strange occurrences occurred in the house that he had never experienced before. The home became filled with a peculiar smell, he heard unexplained noises, and often had a strange feeling while working on the movie. He also had issues with technology. His cell phone malfunctioned, and his computer broke three times. Ric had it repaired time and time again, setting his work back a substantial amount (Fitzhugh, 2013). In his opinion, it was like the witch didn't like the way they were telling her story.

Ric also notes that several of their filming locations experienced fires in the months after the film crew had been there, including the church in town and the home of the Bell Witch Museum's curator. Unfortunately, she died in the blaze at the front door; it was clear she was trying to escape. Ric says that three unexplained fires in one year, connected only by this story, must be more than a coincidence. He is sure they had something to do with the Bell Witch.

A few years after the movie was released, producer Linda Thornton returned to the cave with a group of people. When she separated from the group to go back to her car, she heard a voice calling, "Linda! Linda!" (Fitzhugh, 2013). She assumed it was someone from the group trying to freak her out, but when she turned around, there was nobody near her. She then experienced an unnerving feeling that something was very wrong, and was left numb from the entire occurrence.

An Anonymous Source

In 1998, a witness who desires to stay anonymous experienced a sighting of the Bell Witch—though this story differs slightly from others. This person and three friends visited the property, inspired by curiosity about the legend. This person spent many years reading about the entity, and desired to see for themselves what all the fuss was about. They went to the farmhouse and found out it was closed. They then went to the clearing behind the property. There, they heard what they described as the strangest noise of their lives. The sound was so odd, this person attributed it to paranormal hounds roaming the property and stalking enslaved people from the 1800s. This person led the group as they walked into the field. That night, there was a full moon that illuminated the entire clearing. This person got a little in front of their friends when suddenly, the entire area went pitch black. It was like someone extinguished the light of the moon. They turned around and told their friends they would not go any further. Something was definitely wrong. No good would come from them continuing their exploration.

DEBUNKING AND SKEPTICS

Skeptics have had centuries to debunk and speculate on the true story of the Bell Witch. Unlike many other tales of hauntings, people have written scientific papers to explain the occurrences. Hours of research have gone into disproving the stories of those who believe in her legend, and some of the evidence is quite compelling.

A popular theory is that Betsy Bell's husband, Richard Powell, was behind a lot of the strange occurrences. He was so smitten with his former student that he was hellbent on making sure she didn't marry her sweetheart, Joshua. This was the reason he began an all-out campaign to ensure that their union never took place. Using "pranks, tricks, and with the help of several accomplices, it is theorized that Powell created all of the 'effects' of the ghost to scare Gardner away" (Wagner, 2017).

However, this theory does not explain the strange physical attacks others experienced, including Dean and Betsy's siblings. Richard had no motive to hurt or terrorize others.

Another theory is that this was a case of "the poltergeist-faking syndrome" where a child causes mischief (Kreidler, 2014). It does, however, seem hard to believe that a child could cause all these disturbances.

Dr. Meagan Mann, an assistant professor of chemistry at Austin Peay State University, decided to view the stories of the Bell Witch through a scientific lens. She began by looking into the Bell family and the records of people who lived in Adams at the time. She explored the circumstances around John Bell's death, which she explains to be the result of arsenic poisoning (Nixon, 2017). This caused strange twitching in his face, which many at the time thought resulted from dark magic, but could have been a side effect of the poison. She didn't acknowledge the remainder of the hauntings, but felt that she successfully disproved the notion that a witch murdered him.

A local psychic corroborates this theory, claiming she knows what happened to John Bell, sayings, "A slave killed John Bell, poisoning him because he could not protect Betsy, then eleven, from her father who was sexually abusing her" (Young, 2015). This could be the reason Betsy was so tormented during this time. Perhaps her young mind could not process the abuse she was experiencing, and she imagined the paranormal experience instead.

None of these theories cover all the circumstances, nor do they successfully explain away each incident;

however, it is enough for many skeptics to believe that all of this is rumor and mythical storytelling.

THE BELL WITCH

Both the mythical and historical sides of the Bell Witch story are truly fascinating. No matter one's stance on the paranormal, learning about such a supernatural legend can be intriguing.

The farm is now open to visitors who hope to have a run-in with the witch. Though this might terrify some to their core, thrill-seekers and those inquisitive about the supernatural are determined to see this powerful entity. You can still visit the home, the farm, and the cave where the witch is thought to live. There are tours run by paranormal experts and those acquainted with the story of the Bell family. This is a popular place to visit when passing through Adams, Tennessee, and is an integral part of Southern mythology.

Whether you believe the various terrifying stories or are sure there is no way something like this could exist, it can be an incredibly engaging story. Many find the history behind the narrative to be particularly captivating, and learning all about the Bell family gives a great insight into life in nineteenth century America.

CHAPTER 2
THE TRAGIC CASE AND HAUNTING OF THE LOS FELIZ MANSION

T he tragic case of the Los Feliz Mansion is one of the most famous true-crime stories of the twentieth century. Every true-crime podcast and television show in America has explored it, reaching a worldwide audience who have become obsessed with what happened. The property has become a tourist destination for true-crime afficiona-dos, amassing as much popularity as the site of the Black Dahlia Murder and OJ Simpson's Brentwood home, both of which are also in Los Angeles. This story also had paranormal aspects which cannot be ignored.

This story begins with a family. Harold Perelson was a renowned cardiothoracic surgeon. His wife Lillian, was described as a caring mother and loving wife. They had three children: Judye, Joel, and Debbie.

At 4:30 am on December 6th, 1959, the doctor murdered one of his family members and brutally bludgeoned another, then ingested pills to end his own life. Since then, their home—dubbed the Los Feliz Mansion or the Los Feliz Murder House—has never been the same. So, who was this family, and why did this happen? What paranormal activity has there been in the house since, and what is happening in the mansion now?

WHO WERE THE PERELSONS?

By all accounts, the Perelsons were an average family. Lillian and Harold welcomed their first child, Judye, in 1941. Five years later, their son Joel was born. In 1948, they had their final child, Debbie. People who knew them, who babysat for them and came to dinners, are still baffled as to why this crime occurred.

Doctor Harold Perelson was not only a renowned surgeon, but he was also a well-respected keynote speaker at many medical conferences across the United States. He gained even further notoriety for inventing a new type of syringe. A child of Eastern European immigrants, he worked hard and was at the top of his professional career. He appeared to be a loving father, outwardly portraying a great relationship with his children and a healthy relationship with his wife.

In the early 1950s, the family moved to 2475 Glendower Place, a Spanish Revival-style house so large it was considered a mansion. The real-estate listing at the time boasted twelve rooms, spectacular views, and stunning gardens. It had a tiled entryway and a stairway that led to the living room, dining room, kitchen, breakfast room, den, and a beautiful glass conservatory. The second floor had four bedrooms and three bathrooms, as well as a bar and a ballroom. While there were also staff quarters available, the Perelson did not have anybody employed full-time, so seemingly this was an unused part of the home. With these many lavish features, it is clear this was not the average family home. The house is located in the affluent suburb of Los Feliz, Los Angeles, a quiet corner of a busy city. The house was bought for $60,000—approximately half a million dollars today (Maysh, 2019).

Neighbors remember the Perelson kids as happy, unassuming children who caused no trouble. Particularly, those who knew Judye described her as being sweet. Her 1958 yearbook from Barrister High School documents that she was a member of the Girls League and a secretary for the student body council. These were well-rounded all-American kids living everyday life.

BEGINNING OF THE END

By 1959, only a few years after the mansion's purchase, Harold Perelson found himself in immeasurable financial strife. The syringe he invented was losing him money. Despite it being his grand creation, it was not the commercial powerhouse he anticipated. He had entered into a contract with a man allegedly named Edward Shustack, who promised to turn the syringe into a marketable item. They planned to split the profits. It is reported that Harold and Lillian contributed $24,496 to this project, much of it from their savings. This seemed to be the beginning of the end for this family.

In 1952, Harold accused Shustack of using a fake name and willfully misleading him. The court proceedings lasted several years and burned through the remainder of the Perelsons' money. Reporter Jeff Maysh quotes a letter from Judye as saying, "My family is on the merry-go-round again, same problems, same worries, only tenfold ... My parents, so to speak, are in a bind financially." Judye wrote this right before the attacks took place.

This was not the only financial strain on the family. In 1957, Judye was driving her parents' car when she got into an accident, with both her siblings as passengers. "Judye suffered hand and knee injuries, concussion, and 'severe shock'. Young Joel had a head injury and 'severe shock to the nervous system'; and Deborah's cheek was sliced open" (Maysh, 2019). The medical bills for the children were costly. To assist with these payments, Harold took the other driver to court, seeking $50,000 to cover the expenses of the accident. He only won $10,000, barely enough to cover the children's medical bills, once again losing more on a court case than he won, since the legal fees exceeded the restitution. This was another financial blow he could not afford.

These issues effected mental strain on the patriarch of the family and his psychological health. He had a few heart attacks, which impacted his ability to work and even led to hospitalization.

This series of events defined the last few years of the Perelson family's lives. The financial stress Harold Perelson felt changed everything. Even for those who survived, life would never be the same.

TERRIFYING AWAKENING

For many across the world, December is a time spent with family. It is a merry season, with Christmas in full swing and the new year just around the corner. Unfortunately, this was not the case for the Perelson family in 1959. In the very early morning of December 6th, Harold Pereleson began a brutal attack on his family, which has remained in the public consciousness decades after it happened.

At 4:30 am, armed with a ball-peen hammer, Harold struck his wife in the back of her head. Lillian did not see the attack coming, and did not even have time to scream and warn her children. While his wife bled out onto their bed, Harold walked to his eldest daughter's room and lashed out at her with the same hammer. Judye was aware of the attack and raised her arm in defense, softening the impact. She survived the blow and screamed so loudly that a few close neighbors were alerted to the horrors taking place at the house.

Judye was disoriented and confused, but alert. Harold advised his daughter to "lay still" and "be quiet" (Maysh, 2019); luckily, she did not comply. She played dead until he left, then ran from her bedroom to her parents' room, looking for her mother. After seeing what her father had done, Judye ran to her neighbors, banging on all their doors until they came to help. Doctor Cheri Lewis, a former babysitter of the two younger Perelson children, remembers this early morning vividly. Judye entered their home, her body soaked in blood (Pool, 2009). The Lewis family was very close with the Perelsons, and they could not believe what they were seeing. From their home, Judye was rushed to Central Receiving Hospital, and then to General Hospital, where she was treated for a possible skull fracture and extreme bruising.

Her scream also woke her two younger siblings. The Los Angeles Times reported: "When the victim's screams awakened two younger children, Perelson told them they simply had a bad dream, his youngest daughter told police. 'Go back to bed. This is a nightmare,' he told 11-year-old Debbie. As a result, she and her thirteen-year-old brother, Joel, escaped injury" (Pool, 2009).

As this was happening, Marshall Ross, another family neighbor, entered the home after hearing the scream and commotion. He found the two younger children hiding on the first floor, uninjured. He continued upstairs to inspect what else had happened, where he came face to face with Harold. According to the coroner's report, Harold told Marshall to go home and not bother him before walking to the bathroom (Pool, 2009). Without knowing the horrors of what Harold had done, Marshall did not think to apprehend the doctor.

Upon entering the bathroom, Dr. Perelson rummaged through the medicine cabinet. In the process, he covered every surface he touched in the blood of his wife and daughter. He searched until he found the drug Nembutal, a fast-acting barbiturate. This is the drug that supposedly killed Judy Garland, and has been a common drug for attempting suicide. Harold took several other pills to ensure that he would not survive, including codeine and other powerful tranquilizers. He left little up to chance. His experience in the medical field-assisted with this, as he knew what had the highest chance of ending his life quickly. The doctor then went to bed and waited for the drugs to kill him.

The LAPD arrived fifteen minutes after Marshall Ross entered the house and found Harold Perelson in the bed, hammer still in hand and covered in blood. While he was still breathing at that time, he would be dead before the ambulance arrived. Lillian died in her bed from asphyxiation—after she was attacked, she drowned in her own blood.

This was how the horrendous events of that early morning ended. Both Harold and Lillian were dead, Judye was severely beaten, and all three children were orphans.

INVESTIGATION

Despite both formal and informal investigations into this case, it is still unclear why things seemed so dire that Harold saw this as his only option. Over the years, both detectives and amateur sleuths have pored over the details of the murders, looking for answers. Unfortunately, the surviving family members have disappeared into anonymity. Unlike many survivors of famous criminal cases, they have not spoken publicly about their ordeal, so the entire night remains shrouded in secrecy. Despite decades of people searching for any details that they can find about the

Perelsons, there is still very little known about them. Due to the lack of information, anything remotely linked to the family has become fodder for speculation.

The police investigation into this case began almost immediately. One of the first notable findings was the book on Harold's nightstand—a copy of Dante's *The Divine Comedy*, opened to a page that reads "Midway upon the journey of our life I found myself within a forest dark, for the straightforward pathway had been lost" (Maysh, 2019). This passage is enough to spark several theories about what Harold thought as he planned and executed his attack on his family. An obvious interpretation is that this was a truly lost man who believed he had no choice but to murder his family to save them from the shame his financial issues would bring. This is not a straightforward path, though it would be one that ended his struggles for good. His actions remain inexcusable, no matter his mindset or inner battles, though insight into his mind is a fascinating part of understanding the horror of this story.

Police also searched the family cars, which is where they found the note from Judye to her aunt that spoke of the financial crisis her parents were facing. In this letter, it is reported that Judye also spoke of finding a job to help her parents during this time, as she found it difficult to watch them struggle. These two pieces of evidence created a clear-cut case for the police. The family's main breadwinner was in apparent financial distress, which was causing him medical issues, and he saw that ending the lives of those in his family would be the way to spare them from the troubles his mistakes had caused. Which unfortunately, resulted in two deaths and lives ruined.

Investigators found that the family had a seemingly ordinary night on December 5th. Based on witness statements from the children and evidence found at the crime scene, the family ate dinner together that night without incident and casually went to bed. The rest of the family was not privy to Harold's inner turmoil, so what happened in the time between saying goodnight to his family and 4:30 am, when he killed his wife?

For those close to the Perelsons, the police investigation wasn't enough. They needed more information, and sought to do their research. The Lewis family is a prime example of friends who could not deal with the tragedy without looking into it themselves. Cheryl Lewis recalls how highly strung her mother was during this time, as she and Harold were particularly close. Her father, a lawyer, decided to find any information he could on his former friend. He found the heart attacks that hospitalized the doctor and kept him from working were not heart attacks at all.

They were suicide attempts.

Suicide is not a marker of someone with murderous intentions, so this does not explain Harold's actions. Instead, it creates more questions. If he wanted to end his own life, why did he turn on his family in such a drastic way? The Lewis family speculates that perhaps he was going after the people he viewed as creating his problem, or that his wife may have looked to have him committed, and he could not stand the embarrassment this would bring (Maysh, 2019). Though it does not ease the pain of anyone affected, this is still the best motive found to explain why this horrendous act occurred.

The main inconsistency and reason for speculation in this case is why Harold attacked his family rather than only kill himself. Also, why did he not attack his two younger children? Suppose we accept the theory that he wanted to protect his family from future embarrassment, financial hardship, and further struggles. Would he not then seek to murder his entire family? Did he find it too difficult to attack his smaller children, given they were more defenseless, or was there another reason why Judye was the only one he came after? Evidence suggests that Judye was the only one of the three children who knew about their father's financial issues, so perhaps Harold sought to murder those aware of his strife.

There is also evidence to suggest that Lillian's family knew about the deep financial troubles Harold was facing. It is not clear if they received this information from Lillian or Judye; however, there is documentation that shows her sister Gertrude Saylan "petitioned to take over as trustee for the children's compensation payments from the car accident" (Maysh, 2019). Without knowing that the family was in trouble, Gertrude would have been no reason to do this. Unfortunately, despite her best efforts, she was unable to save her sister from her horrific fate.

In the decades since the murder-suicide, study and discussion of mental health issues have advanced considerably. Modern-day psychologists have profiled Harold as a narcissist. Doctor Adams, a psychologist who specializes in the study of men who murder their families, states that "many of these guys, these types of perpetrators, are very invested in their public image;" and "when there is a prospect that their reputation or status can be harmed, they suffer a narcissistic injury. [Their murders] are almost like a type of damage control" (Maysh, 2019). As Harold left no suicide note, there is no way of confirming these assertions, though they are the closest thing to an answer.

As mentioned, the Perelson children went into hiding after the events of December 6th, 1959. Though it was initially thought that Harold's family took them in, it has since been found that it was Lillian's family. The children moved to the east coast, changed their names, and have not been publicly heard from since. Despite numerous attempts to find and interview them, they have not come forward to tell their story and have lived their lives in anonymity.

PARANORMAL ENCOUNTERS

Like any story with a gruesome murder at the center, it is unsurprising that stories about paranormal sightings and encounters have followed. Despite nobody living in the home since the death of the Perelson family, numerous people have found themselves on the premises with various stories about what they saw.

Often, the people who visited the Los Feliz Mansion were squatters who knew it would be empty. For a long time, the property didn't have security cameras, so they would go undetected for as long as they wanted. Another group that would venture into the home were neighborhood kids looking to find out if the ghost stories they heard were true. No matter the motive of the visitor, the reports of what these trespassers witnessed are bone-chilling. While roaming the house, people reported hearing whispers, voices, and moans throughout the mansion. In an empty room, whispers would begin out of nowhere. The house itself had an eerie, unsettling feel. Even more terrifying, some have heard a woman screaming, followed by a thud and punctuated silence.

Similarly, some report the moans of a man in despair, followed by the same slow, horrible silence. A strange feeling permeates the house, making those inside fear that something terrible was about to happen. This apprehension lingers, then the screaming woman would be heard. Those who attempted to occupy the house soon found it was not a good place for shelter and would quickly leave. Often, they felt as though the dread of the house were following them.

The mansion was not a welcoming host to any guests.

People who have been brave enough to approach the house without going inside have shared similar stories of the mansion's eerie and distressing aura. They have claimed that just a short visit to see the house left them with feelings of dread and overwhelming despair. Those who have peaked through the windows have also claimed to see the face of a woman appear, then disappear just as quickly. There is no physical evidence of this, as the occurrence happens so fast nobody has been able to capture an image of it. It is theorized that perhaps the woman cannot be photographed.

The neighbors also tell fascinating stories about those who have lived at the mansion in the years since the attacks. Those who reside near the Los Feliz Mansion have had their fair share of spooky sightings and experiences over the years. One neighbor, Sheree Waterson, explored the house one night, curious about what she could find. Unfortunately for her, this was after burglar alarms had been installed. These went off as she entered through the back door of the property, but her adventure to the house was not without incident.

As she opened the back door, a spider bit her and her hand began throbbing with pain. The bite was so severe that blood streaked her hand. She was treated by a doctor for this shortly after. Sheree claims that her own back door alarm would randomly be triggered and go off in the following days, though nobody was there. She said, "It was like the ghost was following us" (Maysh, 2019). Other neighbors have reported hearing the mansion's alarm system being triggered without cause. There would be nobody near the property, and yet, it would sound through the neighborhood.

In his book, *Hollywood Obscura*, author Brian Clane explores what paranormal investigators and ghost hunters have found at the mansion. These reports echo what squatters, visitors, and neighbors alike have said. The ghost hunters specifically focused on the spirit of a woman at the property, who seems to be terrified of something. She is known to yell "no" in distress, to scream, and then to disappear. An eerie silence then engulfs the house. They have also witnessed a woman who stares out of the upstairs windows, then vanishes before anybody can capture proof of her existence.

Without concrete evidence of paranormal activity, it is easy to dismiss the claims of ghosts and hauntings at the Los Feliz Mansion. With such a dark history, it is entirely possible that visitors and experts have heard the creaks of an old home and attributed them to ghosts, or have had overactive imaginations while on the property. While this is possible, it is also difficult to dismiss these claims, as they have come from so many sources, all of whom have experienced similar occurrences while at the house.

In paranormal circles, it is assumed that those who have experienced extreme violence or a shocking end to their life may be trapped at the place of their death. Another possibility is that the spirit died so unexpectedly that they did not realize they needed to cross over. So, did this happen to Lillian Perelson? Is the ghost of Harold Perelson also trapped with her? Though there is no way of knowing what is happening at the mansion for sure, it cannot be ignored that all those who have visited have left with an impending sense of dread and gloom. The troubled history of the home permeates through the walls and hallways, haunted or not.

THE LOS FELIZ MANSION

The Los Feliz Mansion has stood mostly unoccupied since the Perelson family resided there. This has sparked an increased fascination in the home, as it stands to be a time capsule for a way of life from many decades ago. The obsession with the mansion is two-fold. First, there is the fixation on the murder-suicide and the horrors experienced by the Perelson family. With the rise of true-crime podcasts and television shows, the hype around the Los Feliz Mansion has only increased, with a legion of new enthusiasts in every generation. Second, that the home remains untouched has sparked even more interest in the property. A property is rarely left standing with no occupants in a busy city like Los Angeles, so this has only expanded the allure of this house.

Despite its lack of residence, the mansion was sold very shortly after the Perelson family lived there. Emily and Julian Enriquez purchased it in 1960, a mere year after the attacks, though they never moved into the house. Over the decades, the house fell into disrepair, though the neighbors have helped with the upkeep as much as they could. Many of them complained about the unwelcome visitors who unlawfully squatted at the property, so burglar alarms and security systems were installed in the 1990s. Unfortunately, this did not stop paranormal tourists from coming to the home, particularly as it was rumored to be left in the exact condition as the night of the murder. People would visit to peek through the windows of the house to catch a glimpse of the Christmas tree that still stood in the living room, and the rest of the untouched house. The excitement of knowing that you could see how the Perelsons lived was too enticing for many to ignore.

Unfortunately, it seems that the rumors that the house had not been touched since the Perelson family are likely untrue. In his investigative piece, Jeff Maysh writes about several historical inaccuracies that have led him to conclude that these are not all the Perelson family's belongings (2019). His research comes from the photos of true-crime enthusiast Jennifer Cray, who once broke into the house and photographed many of the things she found there, uploading them to her blog. Maysh looked closely at these photos to find the inconsistencies. He points out that Spaghetti-O's in the kitchen were not marketed until 1965, so they could not have belonged to the Perelsons. He also notes a magazine from May 9th, 1960, another object that found its way onto the property after the murders. Most interestingly, he observes that the Christmas tree in the living room may not have belonged to the Perelsons, either. They were a Jewish family, and they may not have even celebrated Christmas. Of course, Christmas has become more of a cultural holiday than a religious one, so this is not a smoking gun—families across America, regardless of religious background, engage in the holiday merriment. As a result, it is a little more difficult to dispute the evidence found in the photos.

All these findings lead Maysh and others to believe that another family lived on the property for a short period. It is believed they must have moved there shortly after the attacks, as the magazine found was dated only five months later. The presumption is that a family moved there, unaware of the home's history, then on the anniversary of the murder-suicide, left in such a rush that they didn't have time to pack the

Christmas presents under the tree. Others have also used this theory to add to their speculation. The house could have been so haunted that the family could not stand to live there any longer, particularly around the time of the anniversary, when the spirits may have been in more distress. Regardless of what is true, that the home remains untouched from any point in that period is fascinating. A family's life was left almost completely undisturbed within those walls, making this a one-of-a-kind monument, preserving the past.

Once the original purchasers of the house passed away in 1994, their son, Rudy Enriquez, inherited ownership. While he lived only a short drive away from the mansion, he chose not to live there. Instead, he used the house as storage, and other than the security alarms and minor improvements to the home, he made little effort to repair the house or return it to its former glory. The home's mailbox was always full, with nobody checking it. The antique fixtures were stolen or broken off, but otherwise the mansion remained largely untouched.

Rudy Enriquez passed away in 2016 and, for the first time in over fifty years, the Los Feliz Mansion went on the market. Despite the California Civil Code, which states that "Realtors are legally obliged to tell buyers of a material defect like a violent death—but only if the death occurred within three years of the date an offer is made to purchase the home" (Maysh, 2015), there was no way that this property could hide its dark history. According to the New York Post, the house was on the market until 2020 and was sold to a company named Luxmanor Custom Home Builders, which has not made any moves to alter or resell the house at this stage (Paynter, 2021). There is no doubt that the story of the Los Feliz Mansion will not end here, and that eagle-eyed observers will continue to follow its story closely.

AN ENDURING LEGACY

Something about the story of the Los Feliz Mansion has continued to interest people for almost sixty years. Whether it is the murders themselves or the legacy of the property, a mass of people still flock to the internet to read about, watch, and listen to the story of the Perelsons. Perhaps this is because there are so many unanswered questions that linger.

There will likely never be concrete answers to parts of this story. Harold Perelson's motive will never be fully clear. Over the years, with advances in mental health studies, it has become apparent that he was battling inner demons; however, certain parts of the attacks do not match up. For example, why did he attempt to murder one of his children, and not all? Why did he not just kill himself? Is there anything more to the story at all, or is this just the case of another broken man who took his family down with him? With so much unknown, it is impossible to imagine that the fascination with this case will not live on.

If you enjoyed this story, I'd love it if you could leave a review. I'd also like to hear from you! Have you experienced anything spooky? Do you believe in the supernatural?

CHAPTER 3
THE STANLEY HOTEL

D id you know that a real place inspired the hotel in *The Shining*? Did you know people are still visiting it to this day to find the many ghosts that reside there? Would you believe the tales that come from eyewitnesses who swear they saw the paranormal?

Welcome to the story of the Stanley Hotel.

The Stanley Hotel, in Estes Park, Colorado, is considered to be one of the most haunted hotels in the world. It has been referred to as a "Disneyland for ghosts" and is one of the most paranormal spots that people can still visit. With hundreds of guests seeing different spirits and supernatural occurrences on the property, it is difficult to dismiss the notion that this resort has something spooky happening on its premises.

Lord Dunraven originally purchased the land where the hotel was built in 1862, hoping to create a hunting ground. However, this was unpopular with the residents of the area. Lord Dunraven left the area, where nothing significant happened until 1909, when Freelan Oscar Stanley found his way to Colorado and saw this location as the perfect place to build a grand hotel.

The hotel itself is a beautiful sight to see. With a stunning grand staircase leading to each floor and state-of-the-art features, there is no denying that Stanley put everything he had into making this a place of luxury. The hotel boasts 140 rooms and offers a beautiful view of the Rocky Mountains. With a stunning white exterior and historical feel, it has since been refurbished to keep up with modern times. It now runs ghost tours, and fans of the supernatural tend to book the most haunted rooms.

There is no shortage of visitors who have come to the hotel purely to witness the unexplained. Even on their website, the hotel advertises its supernatural history and has strongly leaned into its reputation. However, like any paranormal story, there is no shortage of people who simply do not believe the tales told.

So, should we believe the hundreds of eyewitness accounts, or is this nothing more than rumors and speculation about the supernatural? No matter what side of the fence you choose to sit on, it is certainly clear that the Stanley Hotel is one of the most interesting haunted venues in America. Believer or not, join me as I tell you the tale of this fascinating resort.

THE STANLEY HOTEL

In 1909, Freelan Oscar Stanley, the inventor of the Yankee steam-powered car, finished building his latest project—the Stanley Hotel. It was built about five miles from the entrance of the Rocky Mountains in Colorado, where Stanley had spent the last few years recovering from tuberculosis. His doctor advised that he needed fresh air, and there was no air fresher than what he found in the mountains. After recovering from his illness, he began building a resort that catered to the upper class. He and wife, Flora, fell in love with the area and weren't ready to leave it just yet.

The Stanley Hotel was created to be a summer resort, so it lacked heating but had all the other amenities its guests could possibly desire. It had running water and electricity, two things which were not yet taken for granted in this era. In addition to these, Stanley ensured visitors would experience all kinds of luxury while staying at his resort.

The hotel has a dazzling history featuring many famous and prestigious guests. These guests include President Theodore Roosevelt, composer John Philip Sousa, Titanic survivor "The Unsinkable Molly

Brown," and the Emperor and Empress of Japan (Weiser, 2019). Scenes from the movie *Dumb and Dumber* were even filmed at the resort (Barber, 2014). Perhaps most notably, world-famous horror writer Stephen King visited the hotel, and later based one of his most famous novels on his stay at the property. *The Shining* tells the story of a struggling writer who takes his family along when he takes a job as a winter care-taker at a hotel in the Colorado Rockies. In reality, while staying at the Stanley Hotel, King and his wife were the only guests. The location, with its spooky history, greatly inspired him to write this novel (Beahm, 1995).

Despite its history as a hotel for the stars, there is also a dark underbelly to the Stanley Hotel. It is theorized that the resort was built on the remains of an ancient Native American burial ground, and therefore was cursed before it even opened its doors. There are even stories of Native American ghosts being seen on the premises (Arnett, 2018).

The Stanley Hotel has a reputation for being incred-ibly haunted. Over the span of decades, hundreds of people have seen the same recurring ghosts on the property. What is surprising for many to learn is that the hotel itself doesn't have a deadly history. Unlike other haunted venues, there has not been an abun-dance of death on the property. Rather, it seems ghosts are drawn to the location for some other reason. Paranormal investigator, Richard Estep, believes "we're seeing people coming back because they deeply love this hotel" (Earls, 2019).

This begs the questions: What ghosts are haunting the halls and rooms of the Stanley Hotel? Where did they come from? And how did they end up there?

HAUNTINGS AND ENCOUNTERS

The Stanley Hotel is a hotspot for paranormal activity. Many psychics and believers have named it as one of the top ten most haunted places in America (Arnett, 2018). Nowadays, hundreds of visitors go to the hotel in hopes of spotting one of the many ghosts that have been sighted on the grounds over the years.

Overall, researchers and witnesses claim that most of the spirits haunting the Stanley Hotel are not vengeful. Rather, they actually seem friendly. There are few stories of scary hauntings or people being hurt by the ghosts. At most, people are surprised and pleased to see the mystical apparitions that appear before them.

Many different ghosts appear at the hotel. There is no way to know precisely how many spirits reside at the estate, but there are several that appear repeatedly, to be seen by many visitors. Some guests have even managed to snap photographs of these supernatural entities. There is no clear consensus about whether these ghosts know they are alive or dead. Some still interact with guests, while others seem to be spooked by the cleaning staff. Who knew ghosts were scared of vacuum cleaners?

The Concert Hall

It is no surprise that visitors often spot the ghosts of Freelan and Flora around the Stanley Hotel. The couple loved their home dearly and undoubtedly wanted to settle there as they passed into the eternity of the supernatural. Many guests have spotted Flora in the Concert Hall. Sometimes, the sounds of the piano ring through the hall even though nobody is playing. Many believe this is actually Flora at the keys, making music. In life, she was a talented musician and spent much of her time entertaining her guests. Some assume she still plays to keep up with the tradition. Though the Stanley Hotel isn't quite as grand as it once was, it seems the ghost of Flora won't let it be without music. Stanley gifted the Concert Hall to Flora, and it seems to be where she has found her final resting place.

Another ghost which is seen in the Concert Hall has been named Paul. The spirit of Paul is often heard enforcing a curfew to guests. Many have heard him telling them to "get out," and most reports say this comes after 11:30 p.m. One construction worker also had a run-in with Paul. The man felt that something was nudging him repeatedly while he was sanding the floors of the hall. He eventually left because the feeling wouldn't stop. Paul also seems to enjoy having a bit of fun with tour groups that come to see the haunted hall. He is said to be responsible for flickering lights that give visitors a bit of a scare. Sometimes, he'll even flash the lights upon request! Though Paul has hurt no one, it seems he likes to be a bit of a nuisance. Some theorize that the ghost is someone who used to work at the hotel and found happiness there. Perhaps after death, they decided to come back to live among the many other spirits in the resort. Either way, Paul is a popular ghost and is often sought out by those coming to get a glimpse of the super-natural.

The Concert Hall is also home to a ghost named Lucy, described as a young girl who often is spotted in the hall and the basement. There is no confirmed story of who Lucy was when she was alive, though some believe that she was potentially a runaway or a home-less person who found a home at the hotel for a brief period of time (Anas, 2020). An alternative, more sinister theory, is that she was a young girl who snuck into the hotel and was caught spying on the construc-tion plans. According to this story, when hotel workers found her, they threw her out into the cold to freeze to death (O'Neill, 2019). There is no confirmation of her death, but Lucy has been favorable to paranormal investigators and presents herself to them through flashing lights. She seems to have confirmed some aspects of this theory. One tour group even captured a photo of her. She was photographed wearing a hot pink dress. When the person who took the picture showed it to everyone, they confirmed they had not seen this girl on the tour with them, nor had anyone matching her appearance been at the hotel that day. They came to the conclusion that this must have been Lucy. Others have had similar experiences with a girl in the same, or similar, outfit.

Room 217

Fans of Stephen King might know this room number as Room 237. However, the spookiest room in the Stanley Hotel, and the room King stayed in, is room 217. This is just one aspect of The Stanley Hotel that inspired *The Shining*. However, the hauntings that happen in this room differ greatly from what the novelist eventually wrote about.

In the early days of the hotel's existence, there was a gas leak that almost killed one of its staff. The head housekeeper at the time, Elizabeth Wilson, was lighting the gas lamps in the room when it exploded. She was blasted through the floor and into the dining room below. Fortunately, Mrs. Wilson survived, and after she recovered from her injuries, came back to work at the hotel. She remained until she was ninety years old and was one of the most loyal staff members the hotel has ever seen. One theory is that after spending her entire adult life working and caring for this hotel, it only made sense that she would return there to make it her final resting place. Elizabeth Wilson has made her presence known to many guests, and people have said that "Mrs. Wilson does what she wants, to who she wants" (Earls, 2019).

Elizabeth Wilson has been known to have issues with unmarried couples who stay in room 217. Many have reported that they felt as though there was an invisible wedge between them during the night, preventing them from reaching one another. They have described it as otherworldly, and couldn't quite put their finger on where the eerie feeling came from. Some even described it as a cold force separating them. Likewise, single men have woken up and found all their belongings to be packed up and moved outside of the room, ready for them to leave. She has also continued some of her housekeeping duties. In some instances, guests have woken up to find their clothes folded, shoes put away, and the room generally tidied. Even though she doesn't take to unmarried couples and single men, Elizabeth is seemingly a helpful spirit who just wants the place to be nice and clean, like it was in her day.

The Fourth Floor

On the fourth floor of the Stanley Hotel, there is an abundance of ghostly activity. To start, there are reports of a cowboy roaming room 428. Researchers believe this to be the spirit of Jim Nugent, also known as "Rocky Mountain Jim," who died in 1874. He was famously opposed to the plans of the original landowner, Lord Dunraven, to turn the ranch into a hunting ground. Jim eventually passed away nearby. Some believe his ghost took up residence at the hotel from the moment it was built. People who have encountered Jim have said he is a friendly cowboy who sometimes gives a ghostly kiss to the lady visitors of that room. Some women have claimed to feel the presence of something kissing their foreheads at night, though he has always been respectful to those he has encountered. One couple even politely asked him to leave, and he obliged (O'Neill, 2019). Some have reported seeing a cowboy sitting at the edge of their bed. Even though he is a gentleman, it is still understandably a very spooky thing to occur while staying at a hotel.

This room has also seen other paranormal activity. However, some of these experiences could not be tied to the cowboy. Some guests reported hearing furniture being moved throughout the night when there was nobody else in the room, while others said they heard the sounds of footsteps coming from the floor above throughout the night. Tour guides note, however, that it is impossible to hear footsteps above that room because it is on the top floor of the hotel, leading many to assume this is yet another ghostly happening.

Most of the fourth floor used to be a cavernous attic before it was converted into rooms for guests. Prior to the renovation, the space would house female employees, their children, and some nannies who stayed on the property. This may explain why the sounds of kids laughing and playing are often heard from this area, particularly in room 401. People have spotted the ghosts of children in room 418, and some have witnessed things moving of their own accord. Others have had the sheets ripped from them during the night, and one child even claimed that a little boy was tickling her at night until she told him to stop. Children staying in room 418 have said that little boys and girls have asked them to play games. Some speculate that this is where Stephen King got the idea of the twins haunting the hotel in *The Shining*. Though there are no reports of any children dying on the property, many believe there are too many stories of children being heard and seen for it to be a coincidence. Perhaps they, too, have fond memories of being at the hotel.

Room 407 reportedly has a friendly ghost that tucks children into bed at night. One child claimed that when he kicked off his covers at night, a spirit came and put them back on him before disappearing. Other reports say the ghost in this room is none other than Lord Dunraven. He has been seen standing in the corner of the room, simply observing the guests with no malice or ill-intent. People have said that, similar to the cowboy, he is a fan of women and often shows his affection to them. He has been known to wrap his arm around women and play with their hair. Lord Dunraven has shown a slight dislike of men; some have said they felt a general unease when staying in this room, and sometimes reported missing belongings. Guests have also reported that the light in the room often turns off and on by itself, and that when it is on, one can see the outline of a man near the switch. Some have seen a supernatural figure appearing at the window of room 407, and his description matches that of the former landowner. The hotel staff have confirmed that people have noticed a man in the window even when the room unoccupied, and they have no logical explanation as to who that man could be.

There has also been a man spotted in room 413, yet another place on the fourth floor with ghostly activity. This man is unidentified, though he is described as wearing old-fashioned clothes that don't match the attire of the day. "Other reports have been made of a man's face in a blue ball resting outside of this room" (O'Neill, 2019). This was, of course, slightly frightening for guests, but not menacing or threatening to anyone.

Overall, it seems the fourth floor is a popular spot for ghosts to congregate. If you ever go to the Stanley Hotel and want to see the paranormal, make sure you book one of these rooms!

The Vortex Theory

The Vortex Theory refers to one of the most breath-taking parts of the Stanley Hotel: The staircase between floors which starts in the resort's lobby. There have been many strange occurrences that have intrigued (and sometimes scared) visitors. Many people have experienced random cold patches in this exact spot. Suddenly, it's as though they have walked through a frigid room. Then, it goes away like it never happened. Nothing explains this phenomenon, and it has led believers to think this has something to do with the supernatural. Perhaps even stranger, some guests have suddenly become dizzy when on the staircase, and have described the sensation of someone walking through them.

There have been paranormal investigators who have captured strange photos and videos in this section of the hotel, which they believe is proof of the supernatural beings that roam the area. They have photographic evidence of random orbs appearing, as well as unexplained distortions. Notably, the ghost of the owner, Freelan Oscar Stanley, has often been spotted here with his wife, Flora. He is usually seen at the Billiards Room and the bar, but many have also seen him here. It is almost as if he is still greeting his guests at one of the most important points of the place he loved so much.

The Vortex Theory surmises the grand staircase to be how ghosts travel from one world to another, like a portal between two worlds. The frequency of spiritual activity in this area inspires this theory, along with the fact that guest have spotted many different ghosts on the staircase. Instead of just one or two, it appears they have all passed through this section of the hotel at one time or another.

The Ghost of Billy

The icehouse was a room built in the original days of the hotel for the purpose of refrigeration. Since then, it has been converted into a museum and holds some of the original relics from the resort. Curiously, the ghost of a child has been spotted here a few times by visitors, and has even been photographed. This is the ghost of a young boy witnesses have named Billy.

Billy is said to have been seen throughout the hotel, and is very interactive with guests. He seems particularly in tune with people who have autism and developmental disorders (Hicks, 2019). He often plays with visitors' hair and shows himself to those he trusts. Staff have also noticed him a few times. Perhaps Billy is comfortable with people with autism because he experienced this in his lifetime or knew someone who did. He is an important figure in the hotel, and is near and dear to the hearts of those who have frequented the resort.

The Pet Cemetery

Another aspect of the hotel that Stephen King fans might recognize is the pet cemetery located on the property. The cemetery was made for the staff who lost their beloved pets and wanted them to be properly buried.

There have been sightings in the area of the spirits of two pets. One is a golden retriever named Cassie, and the other is the ghost of a fluffy white cat named Comanche. Both can be heard around the property.

IS THIS REALLY HAPPENING?

If you are a believer, it is understandable why so many have visited the Stanley Hotel. There is evidence of the supernatural in many photos that guests have taken, and the happenings on the property fascinate paranormal researchers.

If you are a skeptic, it can certainly be hard to believe that any of these stories are real. There is something to be said about the power of suggestion. It's entirely possible that people have heard tales of spirits before arriving at the hotel, and have either imagined the noises of the old resort to be ghosts or have outright fabricated a narrative to suit the hotel's paranormal history.

It is easy to explore all the examples of the supernatural, but what do the non-believers have to say?

Debunking and Skeptics

There is no supernatural location in the world that hasn't led to skeptics and non-believers attempting to debunk the stories told by eyewitnesses who are absolutely sure they have experienced something outside of this realm. One should not ignore this perspective, because the search for truth should involve considering all possibilities. It is difficult to know what is real and what is not, so listening to both sides of the story is important.

Just a Coincidence?

Could it be possible that everything happening at the Stanley Hotel is purely a coincidence? Supernatural debunkers certainly believe so. Skeptics who have visited the hotel for their own research have found the strange happenings are explainable by logic. For example, a window closing on its own isn't a sign of a ghost. Instead, it can simply be the wind blowing it closed.

Many say that if you enter a situation looking for signs of the supernatural, you will find them. For example, rather than attributing strange noises such as creaks and groans to be the naturally occurring sounds of an aging property, one might assume these sounds are being caused by ghosts.

Some have also attempted to debunk the photos taken at the property as fabrications or tricks of light. One example is a photo of a young girl standing at a window of the hotel. The person who took the photo says that when they snapped the shot, there was nobody present. But upon viewing the image, there was the unexplained presence of someone looking down at them. "I took the picture, so to see it blows my mind," the photographer in question said. (Keith, 2021). Those who do not believe that this is a genuine claim chalk it up to the curtain being tangled up in a certain way. Others believe it could be a mannequin that the photographer simply didn't notice.

Either way, there is no way of knowing what really happened.

HAUNTED HOTEL?

Whether you are a skeptic, a believer, or just here for an interesting story, there is no denying that a visit to the Stanley Hotel would be a fascinating trip. There is so much rumored ghostly activity that one would be hard-pressed *not* to experience something out of the ordinary (even if you believe that it is only a coin-cidence).

It is rare for a property to be full of friendly ghosts, which makes this resort one of the most unique locations in the world. Filled with some truly interesting characters, it wouldn't hurt to bump into one or two.

However, none have found an answer as to why ghosts seem to congregate at this hotel specifically. Perhaps it has a strong vortex energy, or perhaps it is a safe space for spirits to reside. Maybe there is even something to the theory that the hotel was built on an ancient Native American burial ground.

CHAPTER 4
THE GREY GHOST

The history of the Grey Ghost is unusual, as it is the story of a haunting on a ship rather than at a home or institution. This story takes place on the *Queen Mary*, a bigger, faster, and more technologically advanced ship than the Titanic. Operating first as a luxury travel ocean liner, the *Queen Mary* experienced quite a transformation in its operational years, assisting the British army in World War II and creating quite a track record as one of the most famous ships in history.

During the war, the ship gained its nickname, the Grey Ghost, as it was painted a dull, gray color and could avoid torpedo attacks like a ghost moving in the night. Along with its conventional fame, the ship is also acknowledged as one of the most haunted locations in the world. Now docked in Long Beach, California, the *Queen Mary* is visited by those interested in its history and paranormal tales. Many hope they will see one of the many ghosts that are said to roam the decommissioned vessel.

THE HISTORY OF THE GREY GHOST

The construction of the *Queen Mary* was completed in 1935, and it made its maiden voyage that following year after being inspected by King Edward VIII. It quickly became the luxury ocean liner of choice, with royals and other dignitaries alike praising its speed and safety. In these first few years, the ship achieved many accolades, becoming one of the fastest and most powerful ships built in history. However, this wasn't the only impressive thing about the *Queen Mary*. The ship was enormous and boasted luxurious amenities for its impressive lineup of passengers. It had five dining areas, a remarkable ballroom, two pools, and a few beauty salons.

Along with this, first-class passengers had a special menu for their voyage featuring only the best food available. Celebrities like Clark Gable and politicians like Winston Churchill were some of the most famous travelers; however, the British Royal Family would undoubtedly be the most impressive of the ship's passengers. Notably, this included Queen Elizabeth II.

For those who could not afford first-class, there was the option to travel in second- or third-class, which was an entirely different experience from the wealthy.

These people would sleep in overcrowded rooms near the crew and would not have access to any of the deluxe amenities their fellow passengers enjoyed. Nonetheless, it was exciting to be part of the history of the *Queen Mary*. This was an opportunity like no other, and those who scored a ticket were in awe of the experience.

After just a few years of transporting the wealthy, the *Queen Mary* was repurposed to assist wartime efforts. In 1939, when England and France declared war on Germany, crew members began to black out the ship's portholes and sent her to New York. Along with her sister ship, the *Queen Elizabeth*, she was now a wartime vessel. The ship was painted a dark battleship gray, and all external remnants of what was once an extravagant vessel were gone. The ship transported troops from New York to Sydney and Singapore; it carried 10,000 soldiers and crew, and was an instrumental part of the Allied powers' logistics. The second reason for the nickname came from the incredible speed the Grey Ghost exhibited, seemingly having the ability to outrun any torpedo aimed at it. The ship was so fast that Adolf Hitler put out a bounty to sink it.

In October 1942, the Grey Ghost encountered its first real trouble when it collided with the light cruiser Curacoa, which was also from Britain. This horrendous accident claimed nearly four hundred lives, with soldiers dying either from impact or hypothermia as they were thrown into freezing waters. Survivors aboard the Curacoa recalled watching the *Queen Mary* coming towards them and knowing it would crash into them. The Naval Historical Society of Australia quotes the experience of one surviving seamen who watched the events unfold: "The gap narrowed inexorably as the stunned Watson finally found his vocal cords and screamed, 'She's going to ram us.'". Later, Watson described how many of his mates had been so shocked they could not move.

By the end of the war, it is estimated that the *Queen Mary* transported 800,000 service people and was a valuable contributor to the war's success (Naval Historical Society of Australia, 1998). In addition, at the end of the war, the Grey Ghost transported wartime babies and wives to the United States and Canada. These were called the bride and baby voyages, and the ship completed thirteen of these.

With its wartime service completed, the Grey Ghost made its final military voyage in 1946 from Halifax, Canada, back to England. After it was restored to its former glory, the ship began operating as a cruise liner again, attracting famous and wealthy passengers just like before. In 1951, Walt Disney took the *Queen Mary* to attend the European opening of his film *Alice In Wonderland*. Winston Churchill once again traveled on the ship, on one occasion to meet with President Harry S Truman and then again to meet with President Dwight D Eisenhower. Even Queen Elizabeth II returned for another trip on the majestic liner. These were viewed as the *Queen Mary*'s golden years.

In the 1960s, the *Queen Mary* saw a decline. Air travel was becoming far more prominent, and those who could afford to travel in the first-class cabins of the ship were favoring airplanes, as they were faster. The ship was no longer a modern vessel, and with the world turning its attention elsewhere, the decision was made to decommission the cruise liner altogether. Since 1967, the ship has been docked at Long Beach in California. It is now a popular tourist destination, with different sections of the ship restored to recreate various parts of the *Queen Mary*'s history. Tours run throughout the ship, and events are often held there. The ship also contains a hotel where visitors can stay on board. Even though it is no longer functioning as a seabound vessel, the *Queen Mary* remains an integral part of modern-day history.

HAUNTINGS ABOARD THE *QUEEN MARY*

The paranormal activity on the ship is so prevalent that Time Magazine labeled the *Queen Mary* as one of the "top 10 most haunted places on Earth" (Dobson, 2018). Throughout its existence, the *Queen Mary* recorded almost fifty deaths on board, not to mention the mass casualties recorded when the ship collided with the Curacoa. With this many unfortunate events happening on the ship, it is completely unsurprising that the Grey Ghost has a supernatural history like no other. It is estimated that roughly 150 spirits are onboard the *Queen Mary* today.

There are a few key characters that guests have witnessed over the years who have made themselves most known. For example, there is the ghost of a woman in an all-white evening gown who dances by herself throughout the luxury suites, which used to be called the Queen's Salon. She has been aptly dubbed the Woman in White or the White Lady, and is thought to be a first-class passenger who died aboard the ship (Dobson, 2018). The history of this woman is a mystery, however, she is often sighted by visitors and staff alike. Her spirit seems to float as she dances, and some tourists have even attempted to snap photographs of her. Unlike other ghosts, she does not disappear in the presence of a camera, and some believe they have proof of her existence on film. This woman's energy is very pleasant, and guests have typically had positive experiences when witnessing her. Despite how spooky it is to see a ghost, those who have spotted the White Lady have spoken positively of her. She is seemingly just a spirit who likes to dance through the halls to unheard music, and does not recognize that there are people around her. As far as ghost sightings go, this is one of the most positive interactions a person could have. There are also reports of another lady in white who has been spotted near the lobby, who is seen less often and is likely not the same ghost as the dancing lady.

One spirit whose death is accounted for in historical documentation is that of John Peddler. John was an eighteen-year-old crew member who died a very unfortunate end on the *Queen Mary* in 1966. The weight of a heavy door that trapped him crushed or severed him in half. He was reportedly playing chicken with another crew member when he became trapped and unable to escape the watertight door, though this is not verified, as the reason he was in this door is still unknown. Another theory is that he was trapped during a routine drill and could not be rescued. The site of his death, door thirteen in the shaft alley, is one of the most popular places to visit on the ship. Often, people claim to see John, and he has also been known to leave handprints behind on surfaces in this area. Some say that he is why screaming can be heard in that part of the ship, as his death was gruesome. When John is spotted, he is wearing blue overalls. Over time, the ghost of John has been nicknamed Half Hatch Harry and has been transformed into somewhat of a supernatural monster, though no sightings of him claim that he is anything more than a spirit in distress. In fact, in 2019, a petition was started requesting the official *Queen Mary* Halloween event stop depicting John as a monster, as he was a real man who had a family left behind after his tragic accident. Despite this portrayal of him as something scary or horrific, his ghost remains one of the most sought after on the ship.

There is another young man who died aboard the ship named John Henry, who worked in the boiler room of the *Queen Mary*, and whose death is similar to that of John Peddler. At just seventeen, John Henry lied about his age to work on the ship during the war, and unfortunately died a horrible death. When a fire broke out on this part of the ship, he could not escape and was crushed to death while trying to flee. He died in engine room thirteen, which is now another one of the most popular spots to visit. Those who have been there claim to have heard knocking and screaming attributed to him, and have also seen unexplained smoke. Certain parts of this room randomly become hot to the touch, particularly the engine room door. It will also get very hot in the room, then go very cold. Current *Queen Mary* staff often hear unexplained banging and violent noises in the boiler room, which they believe is the ghost of John Henry.

One of the most horrible stories from the *Queen Mary* ghosts is Dana, who was reportedly shot dead in her room. Her family, including her mother and sisters, were strangled. The killer and motive for these killings are still unknown. Their room, B-474, is said to be one of the most haunted spots on the ship, and many have been scared to visit it due to its dark history. Despite this, the ghost of Dana has shown no ill-intent to visitors. She can sometimes be heard calling for her mother, or found playing. Dana is also known to wander other parts of the cabin and is sometimes seen in the swimming pool area and the boiler room.

Another well-known sighting is the ghost of a man dubbed the Tall Man. This is the figure of a dark, tall man who is dressed in a 1930s suit. He is often spotted in the first-class suites, and appears just as quickly as he disappears. He always seems to be happy; guests and staff say he smiles at them as he passes, and he has even been known to strike up a conversation with a visitor or two. His presence has supposedly been the cause of phones ringing in rooms with nobody on the other line, and faucets turning on as people enter bathrooms.

In the captain's quarters, the ghost of Captain John Treasure Jones is sometimes spotted. John Treasure Jones captained the ship from 1965 to 1967, sailing it for its last voyage from England to Long Beach, California. Sadly, the captain passed away in 1993, and some have claimed that his spirit returned to the *Queen Mary*. Though there are no definitive sightings of him, people have claimed to smell cigar smoke in his former quarters. Those who worked with him have reported that this was a very common occurrence when he was on the ship. This is more difficult to understand, as John Treasure Jones did not die on the ship nor experience any known horrific event, though it is not unheard of that a ghost will return to a place it once worked or lived.

While these ghosts are thought to be quite friendly, some more sinister spirits haunt the *Queen Mary*. For example, there is the rumored spirit of a man who may be found in the lobby wearing a fedora who has yellowing, rotting teeth. Those who have encountered him have felt very dark energy in his presence. There is also the myth of a cook burned alive by his fellow crewmen, and his screams can be heard in the kitchens; this is another spirit that gives off a very uneasy feeling.

THE SWIMMING POOL

While many parts of the *Queen Mary* have proved to have high ghost activity, nothing quite compares to what some have witnessed at the ship's two swimming pools. Several ghosts have been sighted in these areas.

First, there is the famous story of a young girl who drowned in the second-class swimming pool. She is called Jackie, or Little Jackie, and is known to wander this area, which has since been converted into a theater. Some say Jackie calls for her parents, and sometimes the sound of splashing water echoes around this part of the *Queen Mary*. Jackie is often spotted in the first-class swimming pool area as well, and she is frequently seen holding a teddy bear. In addition, there have been times when a little girl's voice can be heard singing children's lullabies to herself, which is also believed to be Jackie. Paranormal tourists and investigators have tested this by singing the songs themselves to see if anybody joins in, and some claim that this is sometimes enough to draw her out.

There is also the ghost of a young woman named Sarah. The stories surrounding the death of Sarah vary. Some psychics who have visited the ship believe Sarah was a young girl who drowned in the first-class pool, while others believe she is the spirit of a woman who was attacked and murdered in the pool's changing rooms. These are likely two separate spirits who share a name. Those who believe Sarah is a little girl like Jackie have often found the two playing together, and it appears they are good friends. Sarah seems to protect Jackie and is a little more playful and likely to interact with visitors. She has been known to slap guests, tug at their clothes, and even push them. Those who have seen the young woman called Sarah have had a darker experience. As Sarah was murdered, they have felt an uneasy air in the change rooms and have sometimes seen damp footsteps appear, leading from the rooms back to the pool and the pool deck. It would be impossible for wet footsteps to occur naturally in these areas, as the change rooms have not been in operation for decades.

Another famous ghost is often found at the first-class swimming pool. His name is Grumpy, and he has been known to growl at visitors who pass by him. He is usually seen at the swimming pool entrance, and people have reported smelling cigarettes as they walk past this area, which is often attributed to him. Some guests have even recorded audio of his grumblings. Sometimes, Grumpy can also be seen or heard near the boiler rooms, along with Dana and John Henry. It is unknown who Grumpy was in the living world, though he has made quite the impact on the visitors who come to see him in the spirit world.

Speaking more generally, the first-class swimming pool seems to be the epicenter of ghost activity. Visitors have claimed to see or hear all kinds of ghosts; ladies in 1930s style bathing suits lounging on the pool deck or children playing in the water, with the sound of splashing and giggling reverberating through the room. All these ghosts seem unbothered by the guests and in good spirits. Often, they don't seem to notice that there is anybody else there.

Other areas of the ship, which have also exhibited a high level of spirit activity, include the *Queen Mary* isolation ward, where any unwell passengers would go to prevent widespread illness. As this is where sick people were confined, many deaths occurred in this section of the ship. Those who have visited have claimed that this area has a very cold and heavy energy. Often, visitors are filled with dread for no reason. There are many voices heard in this area and sometimes screams of those in pain. While highly visited, this is an uneasy section of the ship.

The Vortex Theory

It is impossible to talk about the supernatural elements of the *Queen Mary* without looking at one of the most unique components of this story. While the ship is believed to be highly haunted, there is also a theory that the ship contains a vortex, or a gateway to another plane or another time. This supposed vortex is found in the ship's boiler room, which has proven to be a hotbed for ghost activity.

This is said to be how the ghosts travel from their time to the modern-day, and why many ghosts don't even realize that they are dead. It could also be a contributor to the sheer number of spirits that are on the *Queen Mary*. Visitors previously claimed to have experienced vortex-like energy on this part of the ship.

Some have also said that a vortex can be found in the women's changing room of the first-class swimming pool. This would explain the wet footprints found on the floor and would also be a good reason why so many ghosts are spotted in the pool area.

A particular ghost, a little boy named Daniel, is also part of the vortex theory. Some have seen Daniel come and go between planes, while others have had Daniel stop and stare at them, as though he is aware that they are there, but is unsure of who they are. Those who have spotted Daniel advise he is wearing a blue outfit and moves quickly.

While this may be too far-fetched for even those who believe in ghosts, it is an intriguing and unique element to the story of the Grey Ghost.

STAYING ABOARD THE *QUEEN MARY*

Nowadays, it is possible to book a room and stay aboard the *Queen Mary*. Functioning as a hotel for visitors, the once lavish cruise liner-turned-warship takes on guests keen to experience both history and hauntings. Unlike many other famously haunted locations, the *Queen Mary* staff embraces this aspect of its history and accommodates those seeking a paranormal experience. This includes the opportunity to tour the ship with paranormal experts, who lead visitors through the most haunted spots searching for the ghosts who reside there. In addition, they run both day and night tours, hoping to assist visitors with finding a paranormal experience.

As mentioned previously, the *Queen Mary* also operates as a hotel. While this was not necessarily part of the paranormal experience, it does not stop guests from having ghostly encounters while staying the night. One such section of the ship was so haunted, and frightened guests so often, that it had to be closed for decades. This section of the vessel is called the B-deck and is located where the third-class cabins were. The once-cramped quarters have since been refurbished, and what was previously three rooms is now one large area created for the comfort of modern-day visitors. When these rooms first opened to the public, those who stayed were so horrified that they would leave in the middle of the night, demanding a refund for their stay. They might wake in the middle of the night to find a man standing over them, the phone would ring randomly with nobody on the other line, taps would turn on and off, and their blankets would be tossed clean off their bodies while they slept. Sometimes, guests would even emerge with scratches. The attacks were mostly centralized to room 340, and after numerous incidents occurred, the section closed.

Over time, however, the demand for this room and this section to reopen became too great for the current *Queen Mary* staff to ignore. People fascinated with the paranormal wanted the opportunity to experience such palpable supernatural energy, and many paranormal investigators were desperate to visit and see what they could find. Now, the ship's staff caters to such visitors, providing a ghostly package "including a chest with Ouija board for private seances, tarot cards, a crystal ball, and even ghost hunting equipment" (Dobson, 2018).

Does this acceptance of the paranormal by those who work at the *Queen Mary* invite skepticism? It has been theorized that the staff may be playing up the supernatural elements of the Grey Ghost, playing sounds throughout to make it seem like ghosts are making noises, planting foot and handprints as fake evidence, and even hiring actors to masquerade as ghosts. While this may be true, it could be true that ghosts roam the decommissioned ship, and those who have witnessed spirits and heard unexplained sounds had a para-normal experience.

CHAPTER 5
PENITENTIARY OF HORRORS

G othic brick pillars and guard towers line the walls of the Eastern State Penitentiary. Before being decommissioned in 1971, it housed many of America's most dangerous and well-known criminals. Now a museum and a Halloween attraction, one could almost forget about the horrors that took place inside. Still, the crumbled remains of inmates' cells and multiple accounts of unexplained phenomena keep the memory alive long after its closure.

Believers of the paranormal and reporters love to flock to this prison searching for ghosts, but the Eastern State Penitentiary was more than just a place where people lost their lives. People were tortured, driven to insanity, and murdered in this prison. Instead of being an institution where inmates were encouraged to repent and reform, it was a place where various torture methods instilled fear into their hearts. Many feel something unnatural is lurking within, but none could ever pinpoint the truth of it. Something is haunting this prison, but what could it be?

PENITENT

Opening its doors in 1827, the Eastern State Penitentiary focused on a primary goal: to dismantle and reconstruct the treatment prison inmates faced. According to Dr. Benjamin Rush from The Philadelphia Society for Alleviating the Miseries of Public Prisons, inmates should regret their crimes and want to better themselves. To foster this environment, he argued a *penitentiary* must be created, rather than merely a prison.

Eight cellblocks branched out from a single guard tower in the middle of the facility. These cellblocks housed up to 250 inmates, and there was never a time when they were not full to bursting. This expensive, massive structure later became the blueprint for prisons around the world. More cellblocks were added, but the structural design resembling a wagon wheel from the initial blueprint stayed the same.

It was difficult to build on such a massive plot of land without running into financial hurdles. Upon completion, the penitentiary was considered one of America's most expensive buildings, and held that distinction for quite some time.

Eastern State Penitentiary was intended to make criminals feel remorse for committing their crimes, resulting in them turning to God to repent for their sins. It was a stark difference from the already established prisons, where most inmates were in the same cell, regardless of their background or crime. If there were punishments to administer, they were dealt with in the most gruesome fashion. Their inmates were no strangers to abuse and were subjected to multiple instances of whipping and branding.

The new penitentiary was supposed to be different, abandoning the tactic of unnecessary punishments for meaningful ones. Inmates were meant to be reformed, not face unspeakable torture. So, what went wrong?

Hell on Earth

When sentenced to the penitentiary, one was expected to realize the error of their ways someday. To achieve such an outcome, the belief was that the facility must instill guilt in the inmates. They had to be forced to recognize that what they did was wrong.

Each cell was furnished with a metal rack for a bed, a table, a toilet, and a Bible. These minimal furnishings were necessary to give the inmate the slightest comfort possible, aiming to make them turn to the Bible for guidance.

Inmates' cells had access to minimal sunlight, adding to the fear of their confinement. On the ceiling was a small skylight known as The Eye of God. With only this tiny sliver of light throughout the day, inmates were expected to look up at it and be reminded of God's embrace.

A host of torturous methods were used to correct the prisoners' behavior and force them to look for said guidance. Each punishment differed in severity, but they all intended to teach the inmates a lesson they would never forget.

Solitary Confinement

The primary method of making inmates repent was through solitary confinement. By keeping prisoners isolated from each other and the outside world, they were meant to turn to God to confess their sins.

Each prisoner was kept in their cell for almost the entire day, with their only outside contact lasting for one hour. To keep the inmates from learning the prison's layout, guards would place a thick hood over their heads so they could not see. Eyeholes were only added to the hoods after the early 1900s.

Prisoners were forbidden from speaking to one another or simply being in each others' presence. Even after the main restrictions on solitary confinement were lifted in 1913, they couldn't communicate with one another. They could be in the same vicinity when getting their food for the day, but they were forbidden from speaking. At night, the solitary confinement rules were the same as before.

Not only were prisoners not allowed to talk to other prisoners, but they also could not interact with the guards. When inmates were given their meals for the day, the guards handed them food through a small compartment in their door. To avoid letting the inmates know when the guards were coming, they would slip cloth over their shoes to mask their footsteps.

Instead of the inmates turning to God for repentance, the lack of human contact was enough to make the strongest person lose their sanity. Inmates would become so desperate for interaction, they would attempt to converse with one another while in their cells. Their primary methods of contact were through tapping the pipes or whispering through the vents. However, if they were caught—and they usually were —their punishment for breaking solitary confinement was severe.

Cave Entrance

Also known as The Hole or The Klondike, this method of punishment was the equivalent of burying someone alive. The inmate would be tossed into this hole and given only a slice of bread for sustenance.

With the lack of nourishment and the limited supply of air, inmates often starved or suffocated before they were allowed back out.

Inmates were often sent to The Hole when they talked back or tried to fight with the guards. However, if they managed to escape from there, they had much worse punishments in store for them when they were caught.

The Iron Gag

The Iron Gag was the most torturous and deadly punishment, reserved for those who tried to break the solitary confinement rule by communicating with other inmates or for escaping The Hole. An iron collar was attached to the inmate's tongue, serving as the gag. The inmate's wrists were bound behind their back and attached to the iron collar around their tongue. If the inmate were to move their hands, the collar would tear into their tongue, causing it to bleed profusely.

This brutal punishment became the cause of death for many inmates, as it often resulted in severe blood loss.

The Water Bath

This punishment was most effective when disciplining escapees from The Hole's in the cold Pennsylvania winters. The Water Bath involved submerging an inmate in freezing water, then hanging them from a wall. By leaving the inmate in this state overnight, their skin would freeze until ice formed.

The Mad Chair

If the weather was too warm for The Water Bath, then The Mad Chair was another punishment available for those who escaped The Hole. The Mad Chair involved strapping an inmate to a chair as tight as possible, cutting off the circulation to their limbs. If left in this position long enough, there would be no choice but to amputate their limbs due to the lack of circulation.

Records of Casualties

Over the decades, meticulous records were kept and archived of the inmate populations, right down to each individual's characteristics. There are lists of what inmates did to be admitted to this prison and how long their sentences were. However, for how inmates died, there is no specific written evidence, which leads to much speculation about what exactly went on in Eastern State Penitentiary.

How many people lost their lives because of suffocation or starvation in The Hole? How many upset a warden one too many times, resulting in their untimely deaths at the hands of the guards? Better yet, did anyone record these deaths, or are there simply unmarked graves hidden somewhere on the property? Perhaps more insight can be gleaned from the accounts of some of the more memorable inmates.

FAMOUS PENITENTIARY CRIMINALS

Before the 1920s, the Eastern State Penitentiary housed petty criminals, aiming to reform those who committed minor crimes. However, the facility later took in more well-known names, intending to reform them as well.

Alphonse Capone

One of the most famous inmates at the Eastern State Penitentiary was Al Capone, a mob boss from Chicago. He was admitted to the prison in 1929 for carrying a concealed weapon and spent eight months there.

When night fell, Capone would cry out for a man named Jimmy, pleading for him to leave him be. Jimmy was believed to be Jimmy Clark, one of the seven people killed during the Valentine's Day Massacre, where members of one of Capone's rival gangs were shot to death. It was never officially confirmed that Capone was the mastermind behind the murders, but many speculated on his involvement.

Even after he left the prison, Jimmy continued to haunt him. Capone hired a psychic to help him get

Jimmy to leave him alone, but nothing they did seemed to work. These hauntings, along with untreated syphilis eating at his brain for decades, inevitably led Capone to insanity at the end of his life.

William Sutton

William Sutton, also known as "Slick Willie," was an inmate at the Eastern State Penitentiary for eleven years. He was admitted to the prison in 1934 after attempting to rob the Corn Exchange Bank in New York. The media labeled him as the most well-known bank robber of the era, with over fifty successful bank and store robberies under his belt.

Sutton was most known, however, for his attempt to escape the prison in 1945. He and eleven other inmates made it out through a tunnel they dug, but shortly after reaching the surface, Sutton and the others were found and forced back to the prison.

Leo Callahan

Leo Callahan was admitted to Eastern State Penitentiary under the charge of Assault and Battery with Intent to Kill. Out of approximately one hundred inmates who attempted to escape from the prison, Callahan is credited as the only person who escaped from Eastern State Penitentiary and live to tell the tale.

In 1923, he planned an escape with five other inmates, and they scaled the prison's outer wall with a makeshift ladder. While his comrades were eventually caught, Callahan was the only one who never was. As a result, the rest of his life is a mystery, since he disappeared entirely from the public eye.

END OF SERVICE

After the prison's living conditions were deemed unacceptable in 1913, and due to overcrowding and the need to house more inmates, Eastern State Penitentiary officials decided it would be best to remove their solitary confinement rule. It became a congregate prison, where the inmates saw each other but were still not allowed to speak. The prison eventually closed its doors for good in 1971 after repairs became too expensive.

GHOST AND HAUNTINGS

The most popular claim about the Eastern State Penitentiary is that it is haunted, though the origins of this rumor are unclear. Now a famous tourist attraction, it was no wonder that the public turned its eye toward finding any traces of paranormal activity in that area. The allure of not knowing where it all began was enticing enough for people to flock to the area.

Hearing news of the punishments inmates faced, those who believed in the paranormal expected those tortured souls were still lurking in the prison, believing that they could not move on from their place of death. If these rumors were true, and it was possible to find proof of them, people would try their hardest to find it.

When the prison reopened its doors as a museum, it was only a matter of time before people came to investigate the rumors of the paranormal. Television shows that focused on finding and speaking to ghosts came to the museum in droves to skyrocket their ratings, while tourists came with their own equipment to satisfy their curiosity.

EYEWITNESS ENCOUNTERS

Catwalk

One of the most well-known spots where people have reported witnessing these ghost encounters is the catwalk, a series of long corridors with an arched ceiling that overlooks the cellblocks from above. Visitors and tourists stated on multiple occasions that the temperature on the catwalk changes drastically, possibly indicating that a ghost is somewhere in the area. The television show Ghost Hunters recorded a video of a shadowy figure, helping to confirm the claims of passersby. One tourist even captured an audio recording of a man's voice saying, "I'm lonely."

Cellblock 12

Cellblock 12 is reportedly the most haunted section of the Eastern State Penitentiary. While it is currently a restricted area, it is no stranger to the shadowy figures that Blocks 4 and 6 also experience. Unexplained shadows resembling people were reportedly jumping from cell to cell on multiple occasions. There were also several people who stated they encountered someone running towards them at full speed, but who never reached them. Each version of this encounter differed slightly, but they were all in cellblock 12.

There is also an account of an unexplained figure in Civil War-era military clothing approaching an employee from behind in cellblock 12. At first, they thought the person was a coworker playing a prank on them, but the person was partially transparent upon closer inspection. Before the employee could examine or try to question the individual, they disappeared.

Phantom Voices

People have also claimed to encounter unexplained voices, such as screams or laughter. The words people heard were inaudible, but their intent seemed clear.

Whispers aiming to send chills down the spines of visitors or workers had served their purpose, and giggles echoing down the hallways only further cemented the fear that people were being played with. It is commonplace for visitors to report feeling watched in these areas.

Gary Johnson Encounter

Gary Johnson was a locksmith who worked in the Eastern State Penitentiary in the early 1990s, helping to restore cellblocks that were once sealed behind rusted locks.

While removing a lock from Cellblock 4, Johnson states he was overwhelmed with a chilling, powerful energy that forced him into an out-of-body experience. During his supposed astral projection, he says he was dragged towards the cell and forced to witness the despairing remnants of hundreds of inmates who used to occupy it. Distorted images of people's faces and bodies danced on the walls. One of those figures even called out to Johnson, beckoning him to come even closer to the cell. Paralyzed with fear, Johnson most certainly did not.

There is a wide range of debate over what Johnson unleashed upon himself that day. The most common belief is that as he unlocked the cell, the ghosts of the cell's prior inmates could interact with him. When he was asked about this encounter years later, Johnson shuddered at the thought of what had happened in that cellblock.

This encounter took on a life of its own, spawning a multitude of theories and interpretations about what really happened to Johnson. No matter which version of the story, each always took place in Cellblock 4 and involved Johnson removing a lock. In some versions, there was no out-of-body experience, claiming Johnson was simply frozen in fear. Other versions claim a cold, spectral hand was shoved through his body. While each explanation has its differences, they are all still chilling.

IS EASTERN STATE PENITENTIARY HAUNTED?

It's no surprise that when looking at the tales of Eastern State Penitentiary, one's first assumption could be that the place is haunted. Due to all the torture and death over the years the prison was active, people might believe in and imagine possible ghosts. But what other explanations could there be for what happened at the prison? Paranormal activity is intriguing because it cannot be confirmed. Is there a better explanation for what is happening at Eastern State Penitentiary?

What we know is that over fifty people took their own lives and at least a dozen others were murdered in this prison. These bodies were most likely not given proper burials, with some stating that some people were even buried alive. This disrespect for human life could lead some to believe that those lost souls are still lurking on the prison grounds.

However, while these accounts have reinforced the claims of paranormal activity since the 1940s, skeptics often say they walked through the prison and noticed nothing out of the ordinary.

To some, the Eastern State Penitentiary looks haunted. It's a crumbling structure that housed the brutal and gruesome deaths of a multitude of inmates. For those who believe in the supernatural, this information would be more than enough to conclude that the prison is haunted, but there is often more than one explanation.

INCONSISTENCIES AND ALTERNATIVE THEORIES

Take, for example, the case involving Al Capone. While he claimed Jimmy haunted him, those screams into the night were not the only thing eating at him. His disease's origin is mostly unknown due to Capone's supposed refusal of treatment, but the syphilis that took root in his brain decades before never stopped harming him. In the last few years of his life, due to it being too late to treat his condition, it is reported that his brain was damaged enough to revert his mental state to that of a twelve-year-old.

It is unknown whether Capone's syphilis affected him during his stay in the penitentiary as much as towards the end of his life. However, knowing it was there at the time, the origin of his cries out toward Jimmy could be attributed to this illness.

Another unclear paranormal case is the one involving Gary Johnson. Johnson's descriptions seem far too vivid to have been fabricated on the spot, but since he was the only one to witness them, there is no support for his claim and one can only consider his testimony. However, when repeated by other people, the tale of Johnson's encounter is inconsistent. Each variation is terrifying in its own right, but these variations only make the case more unclear.

Unusual Working Conditions

Eyewitness cases do not always hold up when presented with evidence or even questioned for validity. Perhaps these are the main reasons people believe the prison is haunted: the people working there even reinforce the idea. The museum workers consider themselves to be working at a haunted site and advertise it as such for regular and seasonal events. They hold festivities around Halloween for this exact reason.

Not all workers at the museum have had encounters with the paranormal, but the ones they have reported are memorable. Some cases happened to people when they just started working at the museum, while others didn't experience these encounters until they had been there for months or years.

During the Halloween season, a pair of workers were the only ones remaining on the prison grounds when they heard unexplained sounds. These seemed to be coming from the room they were in, but there was no movement to be seen. The sound of papers and cups being shuffled around made the pair think the unexplained noises were close to them since they were cleaning art supplies.

One year, a visitor to the museum mailed back a bolt they stole from the facility. The visitor returned it to the museum hoping their streak of bad luck would stop. They explained in a letter sent along with the bolt that they were certain it was the cause of misfortune they experienced ever since stealing it.

A skeptical worker was sure that they didn't believe in paranormal activity, but they began to doubt their beliefs after working at the museum. They saw nothing happen, but specific parts of the museum gave them pains and chills: the punishment cells, a closet, and an office. No other area of the museum gave them these random bouts of uneasiness.

WHAT DOES IT ALL MEAN?

To trust these accounts of paranormal activity, you must first ask if you believe in them yourself. If you do, then your quest for answers could end there. You would have all the information you need, and you could join the more vocal crowd claiming the place is haunted.

But to solve the giant puzzle, one must look at its pieces first. To do so, one cannot look at the prison as a whole.

Anyone can fabricate paranormal evidence. When viewing television shows with recorded footage of disfigured ghosts or unexplained voices, there will always be the possibility that everything you are seeing is a result of movie magic.

There is only so much one can conclude without getting a hands-on view of the place. One way to get someone to decide whether or not they believe is by having them experience the prison's atmosphere themselves. Physical tours would be the best, but online tours could have a similar effect.

Eastern State Penitentiary may very well be haunted. With everything that has happened there during the 144 years it housed inmates, those who believe in the paranormal are likely to say the inmates are still there, haunting the place.

They point to the drastic changes in temperature in the catwalk area and the figures and voices people have encountered over the years when visiting the museum. However, these claims are made only by those who believe in ghosts. Those who do not believe in the paranormal have other questions when they think about this prison. How much of what is known is accurate, and could any of it be considered fabricated? Was Al Capone haunted by someone he ordered other people to kill or had his syphilis deteriorated his brain so much at that point that he was delusional? Did Gary Johnson have an out-of-body experience where he was beckoned to a cell by a horde of suffering spirits, or did he make up that story?

The lack of official death statistics raises many questions, mainly about the well-being of the inmates. We might surmise that people have died in this prison from the statements of employees and tourists alike. However, with the absence of recorded information about this subject, there is a possibility those death statistics are missing for a reason.

It is no question that this prison was home to questionable practices. The descriptions we have about the torture methods alone, along with the lack of death statistics, give the impression that these numbers have been hidden to avoid raising suspicion. Perhaps if the public knew just how many people had been dying in this prison, it would have been forced to close its doors long before.

These missing numbers also raise a different question: did they ever exist in the first place? How accurate is the prison's history, and what has been fabricated by the employees? Could the temperature changes on the catwalk result from physical influences, like air conditioners? Could the shadowy figures in the cellblocks be costumed employees hoping to find someone to target? Is every employee involved in some sort of fabrication to draw in tourists, working with each other to make it seem like ghosts are roaming the halls?

Even with this speculation, one cannot deny something is amiss in the Eastern State Penitentiary. The multitude of claims, each unique, makes the possibility of paranormal activity or some sort of intentional theatrics difficult to deny without other clear explanations. Whether genuine or fabricated, there is little proof of either.

Many wonder if the spirits of the inmates who lost their lives in the prison are still roaming its halls, waiting for an unsuspecting to approach. It would make sense for them to be angry. Their experience as an inmate in this prison had them scarred and left for dead. They never received closure for the torture they had to endure, so it's not hard to imagine their souls would still be in anguish. Like any other case of haunted activity, you can't be sure if something is real without looking into it yourself. If, after reading this chapter and drawing your own conclusions, if you are still uncertain, perhaps a visit of your own is in your future.

CHAPTER 6

THE DARK HISTORY OF THE WHALEY HOUSE

The Whaley House is widely considered to be the number one most haunted location in the United States. In the sunny city of San Diego, its history is a dark cloud over the beach-lined metropolis. Like the beginning of any paranormal story, darkness and mystery shroud the events surrounding this house. This location has a long history, with ties to ancient Native American burial sites and stories of this consecrated land. However, once the Whaley House was built, the dark past only continued to haunt this part of San Diego.

The Whaley House gained its name after the man who built the home, Thomas Whaley. He completed the construction in 1857, and the house has remained a famous tourist destination for a hundred years, with people from all over the world visiting the property. Today, there is a museum purpose-built to explore the history of this house. There is also a fascination with the haunted nature of the home, as many claim to have witnessed unexplainable happenings while there.

DARK HISTORY

The history of the Whaley House began long before the Whaley family even moved to the west coast. Near the Kumeyaay Native American settlement, the land where the Whaley House would eventually be built was once a gravesite for the mass killing of these native people. Whether they died from conflict or disease, the native community's numbers dwindled from 16,000 to 9,000 over ten years, resulting in the need for many graves. It is commonly theorized that any property built on top of Native American burial sites is in some way cursed, and this example is no exception.

The troubling history of this land only continued, with one of the most famous hanging cases in San Diego taking place right where the Whaley House would later be built. In August 1852, James Robertson—nicknamed Yankee Jim—was hanged for grand theft. In 1873, the Los Angeles Herald reported that officials thought him to be a dangerous man, and that he and his two accomplices had stolen a boat. After a quick trial, all three men were found guilty and sentenced to death by the gallows (Miller, 1873). With this many untimely deaths, it is easy to understand why some believe the Whaley House was always doomed for bad fortune. With the possibility of hundreds of unhappy and angry spirits trapped on the land, the dark history of this location could only continue and affect the next inhabitants.

THE WHALEY FAMILY HOME

Thomas Whaley was born in New York City in 1823, and was the second youngest of four siblings. His family ran a prominent gunsmith business, and after his father's death, his older brothers continued to run the company as locksmiths with much success. Thomas's life was one of privilege. He attended a boarding school in Connecticut, then The Washington Institute, before traveling to Europe to study for another two years. After completing his education and living the most of his life in New York, he considered his next steps.

He read in the newspaper that the west was prospering during the gold rush, and wanted to experience this for himself. He first moved to San Francisco, then to San Diego, which was much smaller in comparison. But Thomas enjoyed the European feel and comfortable climate, choosing to settle there. In 1853, Thomas married fellow east coaster Anna Eloise De Lannay in New York City and purchased a block of land on San Diego Avenue. There, he would begin constructing his family home (Strudwick, 1960, p. 19).

Even though he supposedly attended the hanging of Yankee Jim, Thomas found the history of the land unimportant in his decision making. In 1857, his home was complete. He built the house in the Greek Revival style, which was very popular in mid-nineteenth century America and considered modern for the time. It was built with heavy brick and high ceilings, and decorated with ornate embellishments. The design of the house considered the hot climate of Southern California, seeking to keep each room cool on hotter days (Strudwick, 1960, p. 7). This was a house built to stand the test of time.

Once the couple moved into their home, they began to hear the unexplained sounds of heavy footsteps that could not be attributed to anybody at the house. They described them like the steps of a heavier, older man. They soon accepted that this could be the spirit of Yankee Jim. Undeterred by this, Thomas opened a general store in the home. He was the offspring of a prosperous, sales-driven family, and had a keen eye for money and business. With this additional attachment, he further cemented the importance of the Whaley House both as his home and his means of financial success.

Thomas and Anna had six children: Francis Hinton, Thomas Junior, Anna Amelia, George Hay Ringgold, Violet Eloise, and Corinne Lillian. The tragedies the family experienced began shortly after their second child was born and would continue throughout the next generation.

TRAGEDIES AT THE WHALEY HOUSE

In January 1858, seventeen-month-old Thomas Junior died from scarlet fever. This was only a few months after Anna Amelia was born, and the family had only lived in their new home for less than a year. This death rocked the family. While they were in mourning, in August of that year, their brand new house and business erupted into flames. It wasn't the entire house that burned, though the store was utterly decimated, and certain parts of the living quarters damaged.

When Thomas saw the fire, he knew there was no way to save his store, though he managed to stop it from entirely engulfing the family home. This short burst of tragedies was a harrowing experience. Anna was still dealing with the loss of their son, and this second blow was almost too much for her to bear. Thomas suggested moving away, and Anna was pleased with this idea. With that, the Whaley's abandoned their life in San Diego and moved to San Francisco, where they had their final three children.

While the family was gone, Thomas entrusted the care of his home to Augustus S Ensworth. In 1862, Augustus wrote to the Whaley's informing them of the earthquake which had struck San Diego. "Many houses in town became cracked. I enclose a picture of your house, showing the cracks, but it looks worse on paper than it is. In fact the cracks are only discovered on inspection" (Strudwick, 1960, p. 28). Despite the letter claiming that the house was only minimally damaged, this was enough cause for Thomas and Anna to move the family back to San Diego.

Upon their arrival, Thomas completed repairs to the superficial damage caused by the earthquake and remodeled the home's interior to accommodate his now larger family. This remodeling also served another purpose, as Thomas created new business prospects inside the family home.

In 1868, he leased an upstairs bedroom, which he had converted into a theater. He leased it to Thomas W Tanner, who had a troupe of theatrical performers keen to use this space. This was the first commercial theater in San Diego. The room housed approximately 150 people, though it was largely standing room only. Once again, tragedy followed the Whaleys, as Thomas Tanner died only seventeen days after the theater opened and the troupe disbanded.

The next year, Thomas leased most of the upper floor, including three bedrooms, as a courthouse. As the house was in Old Town San Diego, this created an uproar for those who lived in New Town, as they wanted the courthouse to be nearer to them. The house, and the Whaley family, received much negative scrutiny, and even some attacks, as a result of this. Though Thomas attempted to sell the house to the county several times, the Whaley family remained the owners for many years to come.

In 1882, two of the Whaley children—Anna Amelia and Violet Eloise—married. Anna was in a happy marriage with her cousin John, who she considered the love of her life. Her sister was not as fortunate.

Violet reportedly experienced issues with her emotions, and at a young age found herself tied to a scam artist who married her with ulterior motives. His name was supposedly George T Bertolacci. In the beginning, it was a celebrated union. The family showered the couple with gifts and praise, enamored with the man who married their daughter, though this did not last long at all. Shortly after their union, Violet woke to find that George had fled. Despite being a married woman, she was all alone. It is believed that the con man was looking to secure a portion of the Whaley's fortune, and when this proved to be more difficult than he anticipated, he cut his losses and left his new bride to pick up the pieces of her life.

Unfortunately, this meant that Violet was forced to file for divorce, the proceedings of which took almost a full year to finalize. Even though her husband aban-doned her, it was not commonplace for a divorce to occur at this point in history. It was particularly taboo that she had sought out the divorce, which led to her being shunned and isolated by her community. In

1885, at the young age of twenty-two, Violet Eloise Whaley shot herself in the chest. Her embarrassment and shame had not eased in the years since the failed marriage, and perhaps she saw suicide as her only way out. Her father found her shortly after, and she died in his arms.

She was the second of the Whaley children to pass away at the Whaley House.

At the time of Violet's suicide, her sister Corrine Lillian Whaley was engaged to be married. The death caused such controversy in the town that her fiancé broke the engagement off, citing that the scandal had caused too much reputational damage. Once again mourning a child and unable to stand the sight of their house, Thomas and Anna moved into a new home in San Diego and the Whaley House would remain vacant for nearly twenty years. In 1890, Thomas passed away after many years of failing health. He never returned to the home that he built.

In 1909, Francis—the eldest son and then the property owner—returned to fix the home. It had fallen into disrepair. He wanted to restore the house to its former glory so that he, his mother, and his siblings could live there again. In addition, Francis inherited his father's rental, theater, courthouse business and wanted to transform the home into a historical tourist attraction for visiting guests. He succeeded in his efforts, and the family returned for the final time to the Whaley House.

In 1913, Anna Whaley passed away, followed closely by Francis in 1914. Corrine Lillian was the last remaining family member in the home until she passed in 1953. Each of these three deaths occurred in the family home.

With all these untimely deaths and tragic occurrences, it is easy to understand why the Whaley family is considered to be doomed. However, this leads to a question: Did these tragedies happen to them because their home was cursed, or was this just an unlucky series of events that befell them through the course of their lives?

PARANORMAL EXPERIENCES

The popularity of the Whaley House is thanks to the sheer number of paranormal experiences people have had when visiting the home. It has been widely studied and reported on, from an investigation by *BuzzFeed Unsolved* to a visit by *The Travel Channel*. Those who have visited believe they have undoubtable proof that ghosts and spirits haunt this property. It is certainly the most famous haunted location in San Diego, and one of the most famous in the United States.

The property's history of hauntings dates back to before the Whaley tragedies, when the family still inhabited the home. As mentioned before, they often heard footsteps in the house that seemingly belonged to an older male and some witnessed the shadow of a bearded man walking through the house. Before his death, it is said that Thomas Junior would be found babbling and pointing to an unseen figure, even when he was alone in his room. While some believe this to be Yankee Jim, it is essential to remember that the house was built on top of a Native American grave-yard, so it is possible that one of those spirits could also be the culprit of these sightings. Corrine, the last Whaley to die, also believed that she could sometimes feel her family members in the house with her. She rented some of the rooms out to boarders who corrob-orated her claims, advising that they too could hear and see spirits in the home.

The most popular sightings at the house are of the Whaley family members who died in the home. The baby, Thomas Junior, accounts for many of these experiences; people have reported hearing the noise of tiny infant footsteps, giggles, and chatter throughout the house. Sometimes, a baby can be heard crying from different rooms when there is no baby present. As Thomas Junior died a premature death, it is believed that his spirit is now trapped in his family home. He may not have been able to move to the other side peacefully, and may remain in his family home forever.

Sightings of Violet Eloise Whaley are also very common. Visitors have often reported seeing a distraught woman passing through the house, usually crying. She is also known to look lost and confused, unsure of what to do with herself. Once, there was an incident where the police were called to the Whaley House after reports of a woman screaming. When the police arrived, they saw a woman in the backyard, crying hysterically. An officer approached her and she stopped crying, looking up to smile at him. By the time he grabbed his flashlight and moved to shine it on her, she had disappeared. It is believed that this was Violet, as the location matched that of the place she shot herself, and the hysterical crying could only come from a paranormal being filled with despair.

Some have said that when in Violet's bedroom, they are overcome with a sense of sadness, sometimes to the point of tears. Once they are far enough from the room, the feeling disappears as quickly as it came, with no explanation. After her marriage fell apart, Violet shut herself away in that room to deal with her over-whelming grief alone, and it seems this grief perma-nently tainted the room. Violet's ghost appears to be quite prevalent at the Whaley House, as many attribute random cold spots and strange feelings to her. It is no wonder the spirit of Violet is trapped at the home, considering she experienced extreme depression in the years before her death, which led to her violently taking her own life. She may have been too distressed to move to the next realm, and it is possible that she does not realize she is dead, which could account for her confused appearance.

Many believe that they have witnessed the ghost of Anna, the mother, many times. Anna wore a distinct scent, and without knowing this, visitors have mentioned smelling a French perfume as they walked through the house. This has been attributed to Anna herself. She has also appeared to younger visitors, welcoming them into the home. She seems to be a friendly ghost who wants to make her house hospitable to those who come to it. Likely, Anna did not move on as she wanted to stay with her family, taking care of those still there. She had a difficult life, losing two children and her husband, attempting to keep the family afloat when tragedy struck them time and time again. In the afterlife, she may seek the peace that she never felt when she was alive.

Strangely, some have reported seeing the father, Thomas Whaley, at the house as well, though he did not die there. There have been accounts of him in his trademark coat and top hat, coming through the door. It is possible that he felt such a bond with the house and with his family that his ghost stayed with them as well.

However, there is no way to prove any of this.

Much like any typical ghost house, there are the traditional benchmarks for haunted homes. These include unexplained noises such as crying, laughing, and screaming, the sounds of footsteps when there is nobody present, objects moving on their own, the chandelier in the music room swinging back and forth, lights flickering, and cold spots that appear and disappear randomly.

There are also sightings of other ghosts haunting the house outside of the Whaley family. Some believe that a woman haunts the courthouse. Others have heard the sound of children playing who are not the Whaley's. Some say any nefarious behavior comes from those angered that the property was built on top of a graveyard.

The sheer number of ghosts at this house has turned even paranormal skeptics into believers, as it is nearly impossible to claim that this house does not have *something* strange about it.

A TOURIST DESTINATION

Since Francis Whaley himself set up the Whaley House to be a tourist destination, it only makes sense that the home is now one of the most popular sites to visit in Old Town, San Diego. The entire residence is now open as a museum, with visitors coming from all over the world to see recreations of how the Whaley family lived. It was formerly possible to walk through each room freely, though certain sections were blocked off in recent years, and artifacts have been encased in glass. Nonetheless, the experience still stands as one of the most intriguing in Southern California.

The Save Our Heritage Organization and the Natural Trust for Historic Preservation maintain the house. The aim is to preserve the home's history and show future generations what life in the late nineteenth century looked like. Some rooms are decorated as bedrooms, while others mirror the different business ventures of the Whaleys, such as the courthouse that once operated from within their home. A great deal of effort has been made to make this as historically accurate as possible, and it has created an excellent landmark for the city. Ghost tours are also run on the property. Those who partake highly rate these, as many are excited to see the most haunted home in America.

It will never be known if the Whaley family were just profoundly unlucky in life or genuinely cursed by their family home. However, this does not detract from how fascinating their story is and how popular their family home has become. For decades, this home has provided historical context and education to curious visitors, and the Whaley House has become an enduring part of San Diego's legacy.

CHAPTER 7
THE TRUE STORY
BEHIND THE MYRTLES
PLANTATION

Some scary locations are even more frightening because of the truth that lies beneath the myth. Amid all the rumors and stories that shroud a location in mystery, there is a real story to be told. Whether this is a tale of murder, torture, or strange disappearance, the history is what adds to the intrigue of the supernatural and to the intrigue of what is really going on.

One tale that has a wild and exciting historical narrative is that of the Myrtles Plantation in St Francisville, Louisiana. Blanketed by the dark history of slavery in America, the Myrtles Plantation was home to at least ten murders that occurred in the main house (Taylor & Wiseheart, 2013). Now, it is regarded as one of the most haunted plantations in the United States.

Paranormal investigators have examined the plantation and the owners run many ghost tours throughout the property. Hundreds of people have witnessed strange, unexplainable happenings at the estate, and some even claim to have photographed ghosts and spirits residing on the premises.

This begs the question: Is the Myrtle Plantation really haunted, or are people just drawn to the stories that surround it? Additionally, we can consider what really happened at the plantation in its time as an operational estate and which ghosts supposedly stuck around.

Join me as we look into the stories of this interesting yet spooky location.

A HORRIFYING PAST

There is no denying that American history is marred by centuries of slavery and mistreatment of its African American population. There is no way to brush past this when looking at the history of an operation plantation, and I do not intend to pretend that this did not happen. Instead, I seek to embrace the stories of those who suffered on the property and respect the past as best I can.

The history of the location begins long before the plantation was built. The story goes that this estate was constructed on a Tunica tribal burial ground (Nola Ghosts, 2021). In the supernatural world, any property built on a burial ground is cursed, so if a single murder happened at the plantation site, there was likely already paranormal activity afoot.

The plantation was built by General David Bradford in 1796, where he lived alone, in exile as penance for his role in the Pennsylvania Whiskey Rebellion—a protest against high taxes on whiskey which President Washington had to send troops in to break up (Nola Ghosts, 2021). Due to this dalliance, Bradford was mostly known around town as Whiskey Dave. Once he was pardoned, his wife, Elizabeth, and their children moved to join him on the property.

The property was built in the style of a traditional Louisiana plantation, with a clapboard exterior and a large veranda stretching across the entire house. Inside, the house has twenty-eight rooms over two floors and lavish carvings and ornaments both inside and out. It has an enormous chandelier hanging in one of the halls, and two parlors feature marble mantels. There is no denying the property was built to be marveled at by all those who saw it. To this day, it is still a stunning structure with many of the features of the original house preserved.

The plantation was later sold in 1817 to Elizabeth and David's daughter, Sara, and her husband, Clarke Woodruff. Whilst the Bradford family was in control of the plantation, it was called *Laurel Grove*, though the name changed to the *Myrtles Plantation* when Ruffin Gray Stirling and his wife Mary Catherine Cobb later took ownership. They renamed the property after the crape myrtle that grew there (Cellania, 2009). The property

was sold and bought many times over its history and saw several families come and go.

As the house switched owners, the enslaved people on the property were sold as a part of the property. When Clarke and Sara took control, they "expanded the holdings of the plantation and planted about six hundred and fifty acres of indigo and cotton" (Harrington, 2020). The couple had three children, Cornelia Africa Gale, James, and Mary Octavia (Taylor & Wiseheart, 2013).

Clarke allegedly had an affair with an enslaved person named Chloe, with whom he had a tumultuous history. Legend says that Chloe became paranoid that Clarke would end their relationship, so she began eavesdropping on his conversations. When she was caught, Clarke saw to it that her ear was cut off, and she subsequently wore a scarf to hide what had happened to her (Cellania, 2009). There is also a rumor that claims Chloe once poisoned a cake for the birthday celebration of one of Clarke and Sara's children. Clarke did not eat the cake, "but his wife and children did and subsequently died" (Cellania, 2009). The other slaves, perhaps afraid that their owner would punish them also, dragged Chloe from her room and hanged her from a nearby tree."

An alternative story to the history of the Woodruff family is that they passed away from yellow fever. This one is more widely believed by historians, though fans of the paranormal tend to lean towards the story of vengeful poisoning.

Official historical records show one recorded murder on the property. The victim's name was William Drew Winter, an attorney who lived on the property from 1865 until 1871. He was shot, seemingly at random, by a stranger on the front porch and staggered into the home. He tried to climb up the stairs, calling for help, though he succumbed to his injuries on the seventeenth step (Haunted Rooms, 2018).

Despite records not showing any further murders, there is a long-standing assumption that many more violent deaths occurred on the plantation. Perhaps these deaths were not registered or the owners of the property falsified documentation. There is no way of knowing exactly what happened, which has caused speculation about what could have happened at the plantation.

The history of this old property is rich and troubled. Many families passed through the doors, and many people took their final breaths there. With many violent and difficult deaths occurring there, it is no wonder that the stories of hauntings and the para-normal have taken over the history of the plantation.

So, what is haunting the Myrtles Plantation? How many ghosts roam the halls of the property, and what have people seen when visiting?

HAUNTINGS AND ENCOUNTERS

The Myrtles Plantation is allegedly so haunted that people from all over the world travel for the chance to run into a ghost. It's almost impossible to name every single spirit that has been sighted at the plantation. People have been visiting for years, and many have attempted to capture what they have witnessed on camera. Though as always, capturing photographic or filmed evidence of the supernatural is difficult.

The plantation has been host to many paranormal researchers and ghost hunters in the last few decades. This includes a team from the Travel Channel who investigated the story of the poisoned children and attempted to capture their ghosts on camera (Belanger, 2014).

With all these eyewitnesses who swear they saw some-thing supernatural, one may wonder: Who roams the plantation? Where are they spotted? What sightings have there been?

The Ghost of William Drew Winter

As mentioned before, the only recorded murder on the plantation was that of William Drew Winter, who's death was exceedingly violent. It is no surprise that his ghost is said to have remained on the property and visitors often claim to see him. Legend has it that his footsteps can still be heard on the stairs where he passed away. Many, hearing noises on the stairs, think someone is climbing up behind them, but there is nobody there. Some claim the noise sounds like someone thumping and staggering up the stairs, which is in line with how Winter spent his last moments alive. The sound is more prevalent at night, and sometimes people have even heard someone begging for assistance in this exact location. A few visitors have even claimed to see William on the stairs, though this seems to be a frightening experience. He is said to appear as a dying man, after all.

Like with any ghost story, there is an element of mythology that changed the narrative over time. Some claim that William Winter never actually made it to the stairs of the home, rather dying right away on the porch (Harrington, 2020). This means that any noises heard on the stairs are either figments of peoples' imaginations, or perhaps another spirit altogether.

Regardless of what you believe, a glimpse of William's ghost would undoubtedly be a sight to see. He is one of the most sought-after spirits, and people spend time near the staircase just hoping that he will make an appearance.

The Legend of Chloe

The story of Chloe poisoning the Woodruff family is the most famous and well-known tale that comes from the Myrtles Plantation. She supposedly distilled extract from oleanders that grew nearby and baked them into a cake for the children. While she did not manage to kill her punisher and former lover, Clarke Woodruff, she murdered his two daughters and his wife. She was hanged for her crimes sometime around 1823. Some say she is now doomed to haunt the property for the rest of eternity.

Some people have told stories of Chloe taking their items. Most notably, she'll steal an earring from a pair that belongs to women staying at the plantation—she only needs one due to her ear being cut off. Some see Chloe at night in the bedrooms, visiting as they sleep. Those who have been lucky enough to wake up and see her have found her to be calm and not frightening at all. Despite her murderous history when she was alive, she seems to be an incredibly peaceful ghost who is just curious about the living. Those who have encountered her say she has traditional Southern manners and just wants to see who is inhabiting the plantation.

Supposedly, a photographer was even able to catch Chloe on camera. This man was surveying the property for insurance purposes, taking photos as part of his standard procedure. He swears he did not see anybody before taking a particular picture, and was shocked to find that a person had appeared in his photo afterward (Nola Ghosts, 2021). Many believe this story because the surveyor was not visiting the property seeking a supernatural encounter, and seemed very shocked by what they saw.

The plantation now sells a very popular postcard with this image on the front. It is blurry, but there is a chance that someone was standing in the field, captured in a supernatural photo.

People are sure that this is a woman who once lived on the property—even if it's not Chloe herself—because those who have spotted her say she bears an uncanny resemblance to a painting that hangs at the plantation. Some claim to have clearly seen her staring through windows, her features plainly visible to the naked eye.

THE WOMAN IN THE GREEN TURBAN

There is an unnamed ghost that has supposedly appeared to a few guests and has given them quite a fright. This is the ghost of an African American woman in a green turban and a long dress. While guests are sleeping in a downstairs bedroom, they have woken up to see this woman standing silently at the foot of their bed. She is frequently seen holding a candlestick which appears so real it emits a strong glow and even heat from the flame. She has reportedly lifted mosquito nets from the beds to peers in at the occupants. Some guets have said she even reached out to touch them, though she has never been reported as being violent or hurting anyone.

Some have attempted to figure out who this woman is, attributing her presence to either an enslaved woman or a governess who lived on the property and who was likely mistreated. According to her myth, and similar to the story of Chloe, she had her ears cut off, which is why she is seen wearing a turban. Those who have had a better look at the apparition have even noticed a scar near her hairline.

The story says she had her child was removed from her care, and this is who she is looking for when wandering the bedrooms of the lower floor. "She has been seen peering into the faces of sleeping guests, presumably still looking for her lost child" (Harrington, 2020).

Due to the similarities with her injuries and appearance, some believe that this could actually be Chloe. Most people familiar with the ghosts are adamant that these are two different entities. However, there is no way to know for sure. It is entirely possible that two different women could have experienced the same punishment in their time at the plantation. The years of slavery were incredibly cruel, and slave owners would use the same kinds of mutilations and retributions to hurt their slaves.

Visitors have become fascinated with seeing this woman, especially because she is friendly. People have spent hours in the lower bedrooms hoping that she will come and see them, though she is selective with whom she visits.

WHAT THE RESIDENTS HAVE EXPERIENCED

There have been several residents and long-term employees of the plantation who have experienced many encounters with the supernatural. They all have fascinating stories of the occurrences they experienced. Some were frightened, while others had peaceful interactions, but all were left fascinated by what they experienced at the Myrtles Plantation.

Frances Kermeen Myers

Frances Kermeen Myers and her husband James moved to the Myrtles Plantation in the 1970s and operated a bed and breakfast from the property. The couple went through so many haunting experiences while living there that Frances even wrote a book called *Myrtles Plantation: The True Story of America's Most Haunted House* (Kermeen, 2005). During their years there, they claim to have experienced non-stop hauntings and paranormal experiences, describing the typical signs of a haunted house: unexplained footsteps, random voices when there was nobody in the room, lingering perfume that belonged to nobody in the house, and strange noises that echoed through the house at all hours of the night. Sometimes, they would even hear a baby crying when no infants were staying at the plantation. Notably, Frances had a few encounters with the lady in the green turban. She found her at the foot of her bed and even felt her touch a few times.

Frances also reported the presence of Chloe and William Winter at the plantation. She told stories in podcasts and interviews the experiences of her bed and breakfast guests while staying at the plantation, including reports of beds floating above the ground and items flying across rooms. "I had thousands of reports from guests in my ten years there, from hearing things, seeing things, the bed lifting and floating around the room, to being chased down the stairs with a broom," (Carter, 2017).

The Moss Family

After nearly a decade living at the property, the Kermeen-Myer family had enough of the constant hauntings and sold the property to John and Teeta Moss, the current owners of the plantation. When they first moved into the property, they knew it had a history of hauntings but weren't sure that they believed it to be true. They thought it could be a marketing scheme made up to drum up visitor numbers. "For the first seven years, the couple and their two sons lived on the top floor of the mansion while the bottom continued as a bed and breakfast for traveling guests" (Wood, 2018). Teeta says that within two weeks, the family was already experiencing high levels of supernatural events. She would hear her husband's voice in the house when he wasn't on the property, and sometimes they heard the voice of a childhood friend. One paranormal expert explained that sometimes spirits have the power to mimic voices that make the living comfortable, to show they are not dangerous.

The most startling event to happen to the Moss family came in 1993 and involved Morgan Moss, their son, who was only ten-and-a-half months old at the time. Morgan was asleep in an antique bed with iron railings while Teeta was in the office finalizing details for the property's restaurant. She was alone when she heard a raspy voice say, "Check your baby." At first, she assumed her mind was playing tricks on her and ignored it, going back to work. When it happened again, she decided it was worth checking out. When she arrived in the bedroom, she saw her son was missing from his crib. She ran through the house screaming and looking for him, only to find him making his way toward the edge of the pond outside. She reached him and held him in her arms, terrified and wondering what could have happened to him if she hadn't gone to check.

"When I held him, a warm blanket enveloped the two of us—so real that I could feel the fabric and warmth. Then that same voice said to me, 'You need not worry, your family will never be harmed here'" (Wood, 2018). From that day, Teeta looked at the ghosts and spirits as the family's guardians.

The Moss family claims to have often seen the ghosts of playing children on the premises, including seeing Chloe roaming between the buildings on the plantations. Teeta says she captured a picture of Chloe. While there is no solid evidence of Chloe ever existing, this apparition is proof enough for many that she lived on the property.

Hester Eby

Hester Eby has been the director of tourism at the plantation for over thirty years, and has reported countless supernatural sightings. Just like Teeta, she believes the ghosts are harmless. An incident she says she will never forget is the first time she saw the ghost of a little girl at the property.

Two guests arrived and asked to purchase two tickets to gain entrance, and Hester asked if they also wanted a ticket for their daughter. They laughed and told her they never had children, but she saw them walking up the driveway with a little girl. She remembered all the details of the child and was even going to comment to the couple about how cute a child she was. Hester says of the child, "She had long blonde hair and was dressed in an antique white dress skipping behind her mother," (Wood, 2018). Hester was surprised the girl had simply disappeared, and once she allowed the guests admission into the property, she walked back outside to look for her. The little girl appeared again and said hello, then giggled and disappeared again. It was like she was playing a game with Hester.

Hester also claims to have seen uniformed soldiers standing at the foot of the main staircase that could be ghosts from the Civil War. She says all her interactions with the ghosts have been lovely. She's enjoyed being around the spirits and has never had any issues. Hester mentioned they can be a bit cheeky and misbehave at times, but she says that just adds to the joys of working at the plantation.

OTHER PARANORMAL SIGHTINGS

Other than the named ghosts at the Myrtles Plantation, a myriad of additional paranormal sightings and activities have been reported by many. Hester Ebby isn't the only person who has seen soldiers around the house. During the Civil War, Union soldiers came to the plantation and attempted to loot the property. They were unsuccessful, as Confederate soldiers were alerted of their presence and came to shoot three of them dead. Years later, a maid attempted to clean the blood which had stained the floors of the hall but was unable to get it clean. It was like it was stuck there permanently. Now, people believe they witness these soldiers lying in this exact spot on the first floor, in a pool of their blood.

There are also often sightings of two little blonde girls peeking through different windows at the plantation. Some assume these apparitions are the two Woodruff girls who died there.

Finally, there are the classic signs of a haunted house. There are often strange orbs photographed, and people see things moving with no explanation. "A mirror in the hallway reportedly shows faces of the dead from time to time" (Cellania, 2009). No matter how many times it is cleaned, there is no getting rid of the supernatural history of the plantation.

ARE ANY OF THESE STORIES REAL?

There are so many sightings and sounds that point towards the property being haunted that people visit hoping to witness the paranormal. However, as with any of these haunted locations, skeptics are sure nothing is happening.

Many of the reasons non-believers have doubts are because no ghost stories have beFen proven true by concrete evidence. For example, there is no reason to believe that an enslaved person called Chloe ever existed or lived at the house. Sure, the plantation has a horrific history as part of the slave trade and people there were owned like property, but there is no historical documentation that shows a woman with this name ever lived there. It is also entirely possible that Clarke Woodruff had an affair with an enslaved person, however; there is no reason to believe that this person poisoned his children and his wife. In fact, looking at this time in history, it is more likely that they died from scarlet fever. Skeptics believe this story was started to spook visitors at the plantation and grew into a broader legend that couldn't be stopped. Now, it is passed down from visitor to visitor, and people are desperate to see the supposed ghost of the murderous Chloe.

Another debunked story is that of the Union soldiers. Surviving members of the Woodruff family say that this is absolutely not true and that there were no visits from soldiers during the Civil War. The story of three men being shot is just a fantasy made up to add to the mystery of the property.

The only documented and confirmed death is that of William Drew Winter. However, skeptics do not believe that his ghost still roams the halls of the plantation. They believe that owners of the property have either seen shadows that have led them to believe there is someone there and that the sounds of footsteps are purely the creaks of an old house.

At the end of the day, without experiencing the paranormal themselves, it is improbable that a skeptical person will change their mind. Even if they do witness something supernatural, they will likely explain it away with logic and reason.

GHOSTS OR SOMETHING ELSE?

It is up to you to decide whether you believe the stories of the Myrtles Plantation ghosts. If you are a skeptic, perhaps you are not convinced by the numerous eyewitness accounts, or perhaps there is nothing that can show you that any of this is true.

Whatever your opinion, you cannot deny that these stories are fascinating.

Nowadays, the plantation has embraced its history and the supernatural stories. The website openly promotes its reputation as one of the most haunted places in America and encourages ghost hunters and believers alike (The Myrtles Plantation, 2022). They run tours, and guests visit from all over hoping to run into a spirit. The bed and breakfast is also still operational, and many rooms are named after the previous owners.

If you think about the stories told, you can likely perceive why this is such a highly toured location. The opportunity to be visited by Chloe or the Lady in the Green Turban is exciting. Hearing the footsteps of

William Winter would be quite a surprising experience, and seeing any of the children who roam the plantation would be thrilling.

No matter where you stand on the supernatural, the story and history that comes from the Myrtles Plantation are unforgettable. Now it's up to you to decide what is real and what is fake.

CHAPTER 8
WHAT'S HAUNTING THE SALLIE HOUSE?

The Sallie House in Atchison, Kansas, is a nineteenth-century house that reportedly became haunted by the ghost of a little girl named Sallie after her untimely death there. Of course, some have questioned the validity of this. Paranormal experts have said something unexplainable is happening on this property, while skeptics have diminished this as pure nonsense. Despite this conflict of opinions, the Sallie House is widely regarded as one of the most haunted places in America, with thousands of visits from tourists seeking a paranormal experience (Lawrence, 2017).

WHO IS SALLIE?

The story of Sallie begins with Doctor Charles Finney. The Finney family moved to the Sallie House—as it would come to be known—in the 1870s. The doctor opened his practice there, including examination rooms. The front of the house served as office space, and the upstairs as the family living quarters.

One day, Doctor Finney heard his neighbor screaming for help before coming to the house for assistance. They were carrying their daughter and begging for the doctor to intervene. Finney surmised the girl had a ruptured appendix and immediately operated on her. Reportedly, he did not have time to make it to his examination rooms. Instead, the operation took place in his kitchen. The girl was set down, thrashing and screaming; but before the doctor could begin the procedure, he needed to sedate her. He eventually got her sedated enough to lie still.

This took so long that valuable time was lost, and in the subsequent rush, Finney did not realize the girl was still wide awake during the surgery. Thus, she felt everything as he operated. Unfortunately, she died from the shock of the surgical pain and extreme blood loss.

The deceased young girl was named Sallie, and it is theorized that her spirit haunts the house to this day. Conflicting reports claim that Sallie's surgery and resulting death happened in the basement, where Doctor Finney traditionally consulted and operated. This is a popular theory, as the basement of the house has been said to be one of the most haunted spots on the premises. However, there is no evidence of either surgery in historical documentation, so there is no way to say for sure the event even occurred.

There is little to no proof that Sallie was a young girl in Atchison at all. No records show that a girl died in the Finney house, and journalists Fahrlander and Vickers report anthropologist Sean Daley as saying there was never a young girl by that name who lived in the town. He asserts that there was no paranormal activity associated with the house until the 1990s, though even he has witnessed unusual and unexplained activity on the property. He does not claim that it is impossible that the house is haunted, just that there is no proof of Sallie's existence. However, this could be because her life and death documentation may have been lost in the many years since, or because her family was poor and never documented her at all. Of course, nineteenth century record-keeping was not nearly as advanced or thorough as it is now.

The last Finney of the family lived in the house until 1947, when it was sold and passed onto new owners.

People have reported many stories about Sallie over the years. She was first thought to be a peaceful spirit, but there have been stories of visitors leaving the house with scratches and bruises. These acts of violence are viewed by some as being demonic in nature and have added to the celebrity of the Sallie House. Nonetheless, unexplained movements have been reported, like stuffed toys moving on their own and photos being turned upside down. For those who have visited, it is undeniable that something strange is happening at the Sallie House.

THE PICKMANS

While the ghost of the Sallie House has a long history, the story gained popularity in the 1990s when the Pickman family moved in. Newlyweds Debra and Tony Pickman moved into the house in 1993, while Debra was pregnant with their son. At first, things seemed perfectly normal in their new home. Their lives were very exciting; they were blissfully anticipating the birth of their first child. There was nothing out of the ordinary until something attacked Tony in his own home. While the Pickmans had noticed unusual events in their home before the attacks began, it was only afterward that they understood there was another entity in their home.

It is important to note that the Pickmans' experience in the Sallie House was so harrowing it drove Debra to write a book about it, titled *The Sallie House Haunting: A True Story*, where she chronicles the family's ordeal with the spirit residing in their home. Debra includes passages from her journal from this time and photos of their lives, attempting to prove that they experienced a ghost living with them. A lot of her first-hand experience informs our knowledge of the goings-on in this house. In addition to this, the family has spoken publicly about their ordeal. Debra and Tony's story has been read by hundreds of people worldwide and has enticed many to research the paranormal. Having a first-hand account of something so strange makes it easier to understand how these things occur.

Debra writes that while she was a paranormal believer long before the events at the Sallie House, her husband was not. Tony was incredibly skeptical and would not easily believe that the house was haunted. However, over the two years they lived in the home, Tony no longer claimed skepticism as his perception of spirits and demons changed forever. The Pickmans have since become paranormal researchers and have spoken at conferences about their experiences.

ABNORMAL BEHAVIOR

Before any attacks started, the Pickmans noticed abnormal behavior in the house. Certain spots in the home were often freezing with no explanation for the temperature drop. The house did not have any centralized air conditioning, so the change struck them as very odd.

Debra speaks specifically about the first time the presence of another being truly shook her. On a hot night in the third trimester of her pregnancy, a blood-curdling scream awakened her. Then, she heard the sound of someone running down the stairs of the house. In her sleepy haze, she assumed someone had broken into the home and attempted to sit up, but what felt like a heavy object struck her in the face. This chilled her to the bone, and she screamed as well, waking Tony, who was sleeping next to her. Once awake, Tony also started screaming, though it was unclear if he was attacked as well. They did not stop until they realized they had no idea what they were screaming about (Pickman, 2010, p. 25).

The Pickmans also noticed that technology in the home did not work as designed, particularly in the kitchen. For example, the time displayed on their oven would inexplicably change, and digital timers they set would malfunction. They began to make special note of this, paying close attention to how the times would vary and found the clocks would go from displaying four minutes left to fourteen minutes and back again.

Additionally, there were of course the classic hallmarks of a haunted house. There was unexplained stomping through the house, knocks, and thuds when there was no one present, and the sounds of furniture moving. Dogs would bark at nothing, and cats would become suddenly frightened and run out of the room. Cold spots continued to appear at random, and the Pickmans would even feel someone brush past them from time to time.

Once the Pickmans' son was born, paranormal activity began to centralize in his room. Toys would be moved from their spots and the bedroom light would switch on randomly. A neighbor once asked the Pickmans why they kept the light on in the nursery all the time, especially as they had a small baby living in the house. This baffled them, as they turned it off every night. Their son, a happy baby, would often be found playing on his own, smiling and babbling into thin air as though he were talking to someone. They would sometimes hear the baby giggling while alone. Debra once found his toys arranged in a circle in the middle of the room. Neither she nor her husband had created this formation. This incident caused an uneasy feeling, and they cleaned up the toys, switched off the light, and went downstairs. When checking on the child later, they were horrified to find the light was on again. Also, a stuffed bear was back on the floor where the circle had been. As their son was a newborn and there were no other people in the house, it made no sense how this had happened.

The first sighting of a ghost came from Tony, who claims that he saw a young girl in the home wearing an 1800s-style white dress. The presence confused him, but could not deny what he saw with his own eyes. The first place he ever spotted her was the kitchen—the suspected location of Sallie's untimely and painful death. He ran to his wife, pale-faced, and frantically told her he had seen something, then sketched out a picture of a girl. This drawing made its way to a neighbor, who commented that his house's former residents had a daughter whose imaginary friend was named Sallie. Later, this girl confirmed the drawing strongly resembled her friend.

Around this same time, Debra convinced Tony that they needed to bring a psychic to the house to help them figure out what was happening. Tony was previously hesitant, but at that time conceded and a psychic came to visit. The local psychic sensed a young girl named Sallie, who had died on the property and was especially comfortable in the nursery as she felt the safest there. The Pickmans agreed with this assertion, as they had often had paranormal experiences there. The Pickmans and their friends and neighbors would refer to the ghost as Sallie from that day on.

THE ATTACKS

Debra and the baby were spared from any attacks by the ghost, while Tony suffered the most. Some suspect that Sallie only attacked men, as her death purportedly came at the hands of Charles Finney. She likely blamed men for how she died and would take her revenge on any male that visited the home. She perhaps felt unsafe in their presence and would therefore lash out. Sallie's other activity, such as moving objects, were entirely peaceful, and her attacks would only come when she seemed to be angered or disturbed. As she was so young at the time of her death, this made her particularly dangerous and unpredictable. It is believed in the paranormal community that young ghosts are the most powerful.

The Pickman family experienced many disturbing things in the two years that they lived in the Sallie House, though Tony bore the brunt of any violence. This began with Tony being repeatedly scratched by an unseen force. This happened so many times that he caught it on camera, where it was clear that nothing was touching him, yet marks and scratches appeared on his body. This would often happen when he was either entering or leaving the house, sometimes finding himself bruised by the force of the attack. If another male were to visit, they would sometimes experience the same sensation. Tony would ignore the girl, not acknowledging when she became present, hoping this would stop the attacks—but this often had the opposite effect. Debra tells one story of Sallie biting Tony on the back of the thigh. He had been alone, lying on the couch in the living room, when this took place. The resulting wound could not otherwise be explained, as their son was only a few months old with no teeth.

There is also a story of Tony waking up after hearing people in the house whispering through the walls. He felt a surge of panic and was unable to move, paralyzed in his bed. The whispers grew louder and louder and became more frantic, until suddenly he felt as though he were being strangled. Then, after a few moments, the sensation disappeared, as did the noises.

If people attempted to visit the Pickmans' basement, bricks would sporadically come flying towards them as if someone were throwing them. There has been no conclusive explanation as to why this happens. However, this also adds weight to the theory that Sallie died in the basement. Her apparent refusal to allow anybody to visit this spot could prove that she was looking to guard it against anyone, perhaps so that they would not suffer the same pain she once did.

Some people have been critical of the Pickmans' behavior towards Sallie, claiming that they invited her in and made her feel welcome rather than trying to deter the ghost. It is reported that they gave her gifts, kept out toys which she liked, and left lights on in rooms to keep her comfortable. Perhaps they thought this would keep the ghost at peace and less likely to hurt them or destroy their belongings. The ghost had something to play with by leaving out toys and would not need to amuse itself in other ways. Despite attacking Tony and their visitors, the Pickmans wanted to make peace with this entity in their home.

GHOST OF A YOUNG GIRL OR A DEMON?

Some of the more unusual parts of the story of the Sallie House are the reports of how dangerous and physically violent the spirit could be. Often, elements of the attacks on the Pickmans seemed more demonic than ghost-like. Aside from the attacks on Tony, the ghost would ignite fires out of nowhere, which is typically a sign of something much darker than an average haunting. Along with this, photos would be turned upside down, and reports of objects both levitating and moving on their own have led some to believe that something more sinister was happening in this house.

Despite what the Pickmans and others saw, there is still reason to believe that the Sallie House could be haunted by a demon rather than the innocent ghost of a young girl. This demon could be masquerading as a sweet little girl rather than this being Sallie herself. Some of the Pickmans' testimony about this time could go a long way to support this idea. For example, they complained they often smelled something foul in the house and could not find the source. They described it as a scent of burning sulfur. It is widely believed that the presence of a demon can be identified by such a smell, with theorists attributing the smell of sulfur to hell and dark spirits (Kroonenberg, 2013).

Psychics who have visited the house have had varied experiences and reported different findings. Some have determined that the spirit is, in fact, a seven-year-old girl who complains of pain and discomfort around her stomach and abdomen, and who does not seem violent. They believe that this is not a harmful spirit, but rather a trapped soul who died an untimely death. Others have found the exact opposite, advising that the house had a very dark presence and that it was feeding off the terror and anxiety inflicted upon the living. The spirit or demon was found mainly around the back of the home and in the basement where the brick attacks occurred. They believe the demon was there to cause harm.

Much evidence has been gathered over the years from the Sallie House. This includes photos and videos of paranormal activity. For example, one picture that supports the demon theory exhibits the silhouette of a young girl standing at a window with a horned demon behind her. This is viewed by some as proof that the demon is impersonating an innocent child for its sinister acts.

A decade after leaving the house, the Pickmans returned with a team of paranormal investigators to assess the property. Once again, Tony became the target of an attack and was thrown back about four feet and pinned to the ground, unable to get up. The investigators called out, "In the name of God, let him go." At this, he was released.

Nonetheless, the Pickmans maintain the ghost wasn't necessarily a demon, as they remained there even with a very young baby. They would have left immediately if their son had been threatened, and he never was. The Pickman family also have said that the ghost they saw did not look frightening; they found her to look sweet or innocent. However, this does not prove that it was not a demon, as some argue it could have taken any form to achieve its goal.

So, what is haunting the Sallie House? Is it the ghost of a frightened young girl whose life was cut short, or something much more sinister? There is also speculation that the Pickmans made up much of this story, seeking to capitalize on the fame and make some fortune. Skeptics view Debra's book as proof of this, as well as the Pickmans' presence in paranormal circles, their speaking appearances, and their many interviews about their time in the home. However, even if the Pickmans financially gained from their experience, some find it difficult to deny the validity of the evidence they collected over the two years they lived there.

VISITING THE SALLIE HOUSE

It is now possible to visit the Sallie House in Atchison and experience the haunting yourself. As the house is believed to be so heavily haunted by a ghost who is sometimes violent, visitors must sign a waiver in case of injury. While there have been no confirmed attacks on guests since 1993, every precaution is taken to ensure that those in the house remain safe during their time there. Not only can you tour the Sallie House during the day, but you can also book to stay overnight and have the entire experience of the haunting. This has become a popular option for thrill-seekers and fans of the paranormal, especially around Halloween, when ghost activity is said to be at an all-time high.

The best part about visiting the Sallie House is drawing your own conclusion about what is happening on the premises. Visitors can decide whether they think something dark resides there, or that the tale has all been made up to encourage further visitors.

CONCLUSIONS

Many find stories of hauntings and paranormal activity like these to be interesting no matter their stance on the validity of the claims. Even those skeptical of spirits and the supernatural might find entertainment in the history behind the myths. By examining these stories, it is clear that over the course of history, people have vehemently believed in the paranormal. Some of these events are so difficult to explain that some find it hard to believe anything else. In each of these stories, people experience terrible misfortunes. Often there is an untimely and gruesome death, and frequently entire families are involved in the horrors. From the Perelsons to the Whaleys, families all over America have been through dark events which have not been forgotten.

It is clear in these stories that the cause of death and circumstances of tragedy relate to claims of paranormal experiences that follow. Sallie died a painful and untimely death. Therefore, she took out her rage on men who visited the home. Demon or not, the reason behind her targeted attacks seems obvious. A person who did not die a painful death, like Anna Whaley, proves to be a more welcoming ghost. Anna invites guests into her home, looking to make them comfortable. Anna's life was marred with tragedy and she grieved the death of two of her own children, so her spirit is overcompensating for what she lost in her life.

The screams of Lillian Perelson are loud, as her husband unexpectedly attacked her. The playful nature of Jackie on the Grey Ghost shows that a young spirit may not recognize what has happened to them, as she is often heard calling for her parents or singing to passersby. The story of Anna Ecklund shows how abuse and other horrific acts can lead to unexplained behavior, in her case leading those around her to believe that she was possessed by the devil. History and stories of the paranormal are intricately entwined. Everything we suspect about the supernatural comes from this history, which should not be forgotten.

The best thing about looking back on history is learning from it, which is precisely why some of the horrible practices found throughout these stories no longer happen. Surgeries for children are a lot safer, the conversation around mental health is more prevalent, women are no longer shunned for being divorced, safety on large ships is well monitored to prevent drownings and accidents, and exorcisms have been outlawed. While we read about these stories with great interest, we should also learn from them.

Thank you very much for joining me on this journey as I reflect on some of the best ghost stories in America. I hope that you have enjoyed exploring the haunted locations, paranormal encounters, and demonic possessions with me.

DID YOU ENJOY GHOST STORIES?

Before you go, I'd like to say *"thank you"* for purchasing my book. You could have picked from dozens of books on the paranormal, but you took the chance with this one. Now. I'd like to ask for a *small favor*.

As an independent author with a small marketing budget, reviews are my livelihood on this platform. If you enjoyed this book, **I'd really appreciate it if you leave your honest feedback**. I'd love to know what your favorite supernatural myth is and if you've ever experienced the paranormal.

ABOUT H.J. TIDY

As a writer, H.J. Tidy is committed to introducing his readers to some of the most unusual darker variety of true stories.

H.J. Tidy currently has five titles; all sold through Amazon. His best-selling Amazon Ghost Stories series is a selection of short stories of strange events that explores allegedly haunted locations, urban legends, and odd encounters that have taken place throughout the world. At the same time, True Crime Stories is a slight departure from his main interest but tells of some of the most incredible and mysterious true crime events.

MORE BOOKS BY H.J. TIDY

MY CREEPY PARANORMAL STORY: Scary Stories Inspired by Real Encounters with Ghosts, Creatures. and the Unknown.

A Collection of True Crime Horror Stories: Chilling Personal Accounts, of Murders, Disappearances, and Serial Killers

True Crime Stories: Twisted Tales of True Crime: Murders, Disappearances, and Serial Killers.

REFERENCES

Dalrymple, L. (2013 October 24). *Is Eastern State Penitentiary Really Haunted? NPR.*
https://www.npr.org/2013/10/24/232234570/is-eastern-state-penitentiary-really-haunted

Ellis, P. (2020 May 14). *The True Story of Al Capone's Later Life, Including How He Died. Men's Health.*
https://www.menshealth.com/entertainment/a32461994/al-capone-death-syphilis/

Haunted Prison - The True Haunting of Eastern State Penitentiary. (n.d.). Haunted Places To Go.
https://www.haunted-places-to-go.com/haunted-prison.html

History of Eastern State. (n.d.). Eastern State Penitentiary Historic Site.

https://www.easternstate.org/research/history-eastern-state

Logue, J. (2017 October 25). *Is Eastern State Penitentiary really haunted? Metro Philadelphia.*
https://metrophiladelphia.com/is-eastern-state-penitentiary-really-haunted/

Nealon, T. (2020 May 19). *The Haunted Eastern State Penitentiary. Ghost City Tours.*
https://ghostcitytours.com/philadelphia/haunted-philadelphia/eastern-state-penitentiary/

The Prisoners Haunting Eastern State Penitentiary. (2019 June 30). *Mysterious Facts.*
https://mysteriousfacts.com/prisoners-haunting-eastern-state-penitentiary/

Anas, B. (2020 April 4). *Would you spend a night in The Stanley's most haunted rooms? TripSavvy.*
https://www.tripsavvy.com/the-haunted-stanley-hotel-4108817

Arnett, A. (2018 January 26). *Ghosts, doubles and vortices: Revisiting the Stanley Hotel. Brooklyn Paranormal Society.*
https://bkps.co/2018/ghosts-doubles-vortices-revisiting-stanley-hotel/

Barber, M. (2014 October 7). *Roadtrip to Aspen: Mapping the iconic spots of dumb & dumber. Curbed.*

https://archive.curbed.com/maps/the-road-to-aspen-mapping-the-iconic-spots-of-dumb-dumber

Beahm, G. W. (1995). Stephen King companion. Andrews and McMeel.

Earls, S. (2019 October 29). Colorado's Stanley Hotel offers plenty of haunted tales. Colorado Springs Gazette. https://gazette.com/life/colorados-stanley-hotel-offers-plenty-of-haunted-tales/article_608df8f4-5c12-57c0-a362-e3dc70103bfa.html

Hicks, K. (2019 October 29). The Stanley Hotel's haunted reputation and how it inspired "The Shining." ABC Action News. https://www.abcactionnews.com/news/national/the-stanley-hotels-haunted-reputation-and-how-it-inspired-the-shining

Karr, M. (2019 May 4). The Stanley Hotel (ghost stories). The Haunted: Debunked. https://thehaunteddebunked.home.blog/2019/05/04/the-stanley-hotel-ghost-stories/

Keith, T. (2021 June 2). You decide: Ghost or curtains? Photo snapped at the Stanley Hotel in Colorado recently. kktv.com. https://www.kktv.com/2021/06/02/you-decide-ghost-or-curtains-photo-snapped-at-the-stanley-hotel-in-colorado-recently/

Nordine, M. (2019 October 23). Is The Stanley Hotel haunted enough to scare a ghost skeptic into believing? The Discoverer. https://www.thediscoverer.com/blog/a-night-at-the-stanley-hotel/XvHyVpKgiwAG5awz

O'Neill, R. (2019 October 28). 10 creepy things you didn't know about the Stanley Hotel. TheTravel. https://www.thetravel.com/stanley-hotel-facts-ghost-creepy/

Weiser, K. (2019). The haunted Stanley Hotel in Estes Park, Colorado. Legendsofamerica.com. https://www.legendsofamerica.com/stanley-hotel-colorado/

Belanger, J. (2014, February 22). The Myrtles Plantation. My Entertainment Holdings.

Carter, M. (2017, October 11). A look inside the most haunted house in America. Country Living. https://www.countryliving.com/life/a45181/myrtles-plantation-louisiana-haunted/

Cellania, M. (2009, October 20). The haunted plantation. Www.mentalfloss.com. https://www.mentalfloss.com/article/23051/haunted-plantation

Fitzhugh, P. (2013). The legend of the Bell Witch of Tennessee. Bellwitch.org. http://www.bellwitch.org/story.htm

Fitzhugh, P. (2020, December 13). A new development in the Bell Witch case. Pat Fitzhugh. https://patfitzhugh.wordpress.com/2020/12/13/a-new-development-in-the-bell-witch-case/

Harrington, R. K. (2020, October 24). The history and the haunting of the Myrtles Plantation. Medium. https://medium.com/exploring-history/the-history-and-the-haunting-of-the-myrtles-plantation-6c1190615f

Haunted Houses. (2006, August 19). Myrtles Plantation bed and breakfast haunted house. Web.archive.org. https://web.archive.org/web/20060819122837/http://www.hauntedhouses.com/states/la/house.htm

Haunted Rooms. (2018). The Myrtles Plantation, St. Francisville, Louisiana. Www.hauntedrooms.com. https://www.hauntedrooms.com/louisiana/haunted-places/haunted-hotels/the-myrtles-plantation

Kermeen, F. (2005). The Myrtles Plantation : the true story of America's most haunted house. Warner Books.

Kreidler, M. (2014, January 1). The "Bell Witch" poltergeist. Skeptical Inquirer. https://skepticalinquirer.org/2014/01/the-bell-witch-poltergeist/

REFERENCES

Myrtles Plantation. (2022). Legend of Chloe and ghosts. Www.myrtlesplantation.com.
https://www.myrtlesplantation.com/history-and-hauntings/the-legend-of-chloe

Nixon, K. (2017, October 30). Bell Witch lore spins dark tale, but could science explain it all? The Tennessean.
https://www.tennessean.com/story/news/local/robertson/2021/10/28/history-tennessee-bell-witch-could-science-explain-paranormal/8568160002/

Nola Ghosts. (2021, July 31). The haunted Myrtle Plantation. Nolaghosts.com.
https://nolaghosts.com/the-haunted-myrtle-plantation/

Solomon, C. (Director). (2005). An american haunting. After Dark Films.

Taylor, T. (2017). Myrtle Plantation legends, lore and lies. American Hauntings.
https://www.americanhauntingsink.com/myrtles

Taylor, T., & Wiseheart, D. (2013, October 29). America's most haunted: Myrtles Plantation. Web.archive.org.
https://web.archive.org/web/20131029235907/http://www.prairieghosts.com/myrtles.html

Tennessee State Library and Archives. (n.d.). Tennessee myths and legends. Sharetngov.tnsosfiles.com.

https://sharetngov.tnsosfiles.com/tsla/exhibits/
myth/bellwitch.htm

*The Myrtles Plantation. (2022). Take a tour. Www.myrtles-
plantation.com.*
https://www.myrtlesplantation.com/tour

*The Shakers. (1988). Living in the shadow of a spirit. Carlyle
Records.*

*Wagner, S. (2017, August 19). The Bell Witch: The real story
behind America's best-known poltergeist case. LiveAbout.*
https://www.liveabout.com/the-bell-witch-2596741

*White, R. (Director). (2004). Bell Witch haunting. Willing
Hearts Prod.*

*Wick, D. (1987). The strange true story of the Bell Witch of
Tennessee, part 4 of 5. The Mountain Laurel.*
http://www.mtnlaurel.com/ghost-stories/1233-the-
strange-true-story-of-the-bell-witch-of-tennessee-part-
4-of-5.html

*Wood, S. K. (2018, November 4). Woman shares ghost stories
from her "haunted" plantation. AP NEWS.*
https://apnews.com/
article/6f2498d9f64043ffb8e05487f62fa376

*Young, N. (2015, October 27). Psychic: I know the real Bell
Witch story. USA TODAY.*

REFERENCES

https://www.usatoday.com/story/life/nation-now/2015/
10/27/psychic-bell-witch-story/74713998/

(2019 September 22). The Incarcerated Ghosts of Eastern
State Penitentiary. Amy's Crypt.
https://amyscrypt.com/eastern-state-penitentiary/

Dalrymple, L. (2013 October 24). Is Eastern State Peniten-
tiary Really Haunted? NPR.
https://www.npr.org/2013/10/24/232234570/is-
eastern-state-penitentiary-really-haunted

Darcy, D. (2021 June 6). Wandering The Eerie Eastern State
Penitentiary. World Adventurists.
https://worldadventurists.com/eastern-state-penitentiary-
philadelphia/

Ellis, P. (2020 May 14). The True Story of Al Capone's
Later Life, Including How He Died. Men's
Health. https://www.menshealth.com/entertainment/
a32461994/al-capone-death-syphilis/

Haunted Prison - The True Haunting of Eastern State Peni-
tentiary. (n.d.). Haunted Places To Go.
https://www.haunted-places-to-go.com/haunted-prison.html

History of Eastern State. (n.d.). Eastern State Penitentiary
Historic Site.
https://www.easternstate.org/research/history-eastern-state

J. (2021 February 4). Eastern State Penitentiary: 30 Facts About Philadelphia's Haunted Prison.
Thought Catalog. https://thoughtcatalog.com/jeremy-london/2018/09/eastern-state-penitentiary/

Logue, J. (2017 October 25). Is Eastern State Penitentiary really haunted? Metro Philadelphia.
https://metrophiladelphia.com/is-eastern-state-penitentiary-really-haunted/

Nealon, T. (2020 May 19). The Haunted Eastern State Penitentiary. Ghost City Tours.
https://ghostcitytours.com/philadelphia/haunted-philadelphia/eastern-state-penitentiary/

Punishments, 1780–1925 (n.d.). The Digital Panopticon.
https://www.digitalpanopticon.org/Punishments,_1780-1925

The Prisoners Haunting Eastern State Penitentiary. (2019 June 30). Mysterious Facts.
https://mysteriousfacts.com/prisoners-haunting-eastern-state-penitentiary/
Woodham, C. (2008 October 1). Eastern State Penitentiary: A Prison With a Past. Smithsonian Magazine.
https://www.smithsonianmag.com/history/eastern-state-penitentiary-a-prison-with-a-past-14274660/
Clune, B. (2017). Hollywood Obscura : death, murder, and the paranormal aftermath. Schiffer Publishing Ltd.

Dobson, J. (2018, April 14). The Queen Mary Opens Up Its

Haunted Hotel Suite For An Overnight Ghostly Experience.
Forbes.
https://www.forbes.com/sites/jimdobson/2018/04/14/the-
queen-mary-opens-up-its-haunted-hotel-suite-for-an-overnight-
ghostly-experience/?sh=21d9f942575b

Fahrlander, C., & Vickers, N. (2020, October 30). Haunted
Heartland: The Sallie House in Atchison, KS. KCTV Kansas
City.
https://www.kctv5.com/news/local_news/haunted-heartland-
the-sallie-house-in-atchison-ks/article_f0ad791a-1a26-11eb-
bff6-4382ee261acb.html

Fyfe, D. (2014). Overland Limited. The Campo Santo Quar-
terly Review, 1(4). The Campo Santo.
https://www.camposanto.com/quarterlyreview/volume-1/
issue-4/overland-limited/

Jones, J. (2011, October 30). San Diego landmark is ghost
hunters' old haunt; Whaley House, an 1850s residence rich in
history, is known for its alleged spectral encounters, which tend to
increase in late October. The Los Angeles Times.

Kroonenberg, S. (2013). Why Hell Stinks of Sulfur :
Mythology and Geology of the Underworld (A. Brown, Trans.).
Reaktion Books.

Lawrence, A. (2017). Paranormal survivors: Validating the
struggling middle class. Journal of Popular Film and Television,
45(4), 219–230.

https://doi.org/10.1080/01956051.2017.1302922

Maysh, J. (2019, November 16). The Murder House. Medium.
https://medium.com/s/story/the-murder-house-8bea26f11e5b

Miller, V. (1873, October 7). Hanging Yankee Jim. Los Angeles Herald. Hanging Yankee Jim

Monif, M. (2020, October 20). A disease often misdiagnosed as madness. Monash Lens.
https://lens.monash.edu/@medicine-health/2020/10/20/1381554/autoimmune-encephalitis-when-your-body-attacks-your-brain-and-people-think-youre-going-mad

Naval Historical Society of Australia. (1998, September 18). SS Queen Mary & the loss of HMS Curacoa 1942. Naval Historical Society of Australia.
https://www.navyhistory.org.au/ss-queen-mary-the-loss-of-hms-curacoa-1942/

Paynter, S. (2021, July 9). Inside the infamous "Murder House" embroiled in new mystery. New York Post.
https://nypost.com/article/inside-loz-feliz-murders-house-harold-perelson/

Pickman, D. (2010). The Sallie house haunting : a true story. Llewellyn.

REFERENCES

Pool, B. (2009, February 6). *On a Los Feliz hill, murder — then mystery. Los Angeles Times.* https://www.latimes.com/archives/la-xpm-2009-feb-06-me-mansion6-story.html

Richardson, A. (2019). *Sign the Petition. Www.change.org.* https://www.change.org/p/the-queen-mary-and-epic-entertainment-group-change-the-background-story-of-half-hatch-henry-at-queen-mary-s-dark-harbor?source_location=petitions_browse

Strudwick, J. A. (1960). *The Thomas Whaley House. Historical Shrine Foundation Of San Diego County.*

The Queen Mary. (n.d.). *Queen Mary Story - TheQueen Mary - Legendary Queen Mary Ship in Long Beach. Www.queen-mary.com. Retrieved August 14, 2021, from* https://www.queenmary.com/history

Wilson, C. (2000). *Afterlife. Caxton.*

DREAD: THE UNSOLVED Takes on the Exorcism of Michael Taylor. Dread Central, 3 June 2021. www.dreadcentral.com/news/401927/dread-the-unsolved-takes-on-the-exorcism-of-michael-taylor/.

Bishop, Fr. R. J. (2019, Oct. 19) *The Actual 1949 Diary of the Priest Who Inspired the 1973 Film: The Exorcist. Sensus Fidelium.*

https://sensusfidelium.us/the-actual-1949-diary-of-the-priest-who-inspired-the-1973-film-the-exorcist/

DeLong, W. (2017, Oct. 26) The True Story of Roland Doe That Inspired 'The Exorcist'. All That's Interesting. https://allthatsinteresting.com/roland-doe-the-exorcist-true-story

Hollingsworth, A. [Put the Shovel Down] The Horrifying Case of Michael Taylor (Demon or Bipolar Psychosis?) [Video] YouTube. https://www.youtube.com/watch?v=3MrNhHu-90w

Iggulden, C. (2017) The Exorcist Files. The Sun, Feb. 14, 2017.

McRobbie, L.R., The Strange and Mysterious History of the Ouija Board. Smithsonian, Smithsonian.com, 28 Oct. 2013. www.smithsonianmag.com/history/the-strange-and-mysterious-history-of-the-ouija-board-5860627/

Popcorn, Detective. The Possession of Michael Taylor. Last Podcast on the Left Reading List, 28 Oct. 2018. lastpodcastontheleftreadinglist.com/michael-taylor/

Taylor, T. (2014) The Devil Came to St. Louis, The True Story of the 1949 Exorcism (2nd ed.). Whitechapel Press.

Printed in Great Britain
by Amazon